Taking Godly Care of N

Stewardship Lessons in Money Matters

by Anna Layton Sharp

Illustrated by Russ Flint

Carson-Dellosa Christian Publishing
Greensboro, North Carolina

It is the mission of Carson-Dellosa Christian Publishing to create the highest-quality Scripture-based children's products that teach the Word of God, share His love and goodness, assist in faith development, and glorify His Son, Jesus Christ.

"... *teach me your ways so I may know you.* ..."
Exodus 33:13

For Brad,
a good economist and an even better husband.
When I analyze you in cost-benefit terms, my heart flutters.

Credits

Author: Anna Layton Sharp
Editor: Carol Layton
Illustrator: Russ Flint
Cover Design: Annette Hollister-Papp
Cover Illustration: Russ Flint
Layout Design: Mark Conrad

ISBN 1-59441-082-8

Introduction

Christian schools have a wonderful opportunity—and responsibility—to teach financial stewardship. The love of money is no new evil, but only recently has greed in children been encouraged and nurtured by advertisers. Kids are also poised to inherit the debt-based lifestyle of our generation—unless parents and educators step in. The following chapters will guide students in a new direction, toward sensible and Bible-based ethical handling of their own finances, however small.

Contents

Teacher tips

For a money-savvy classroom

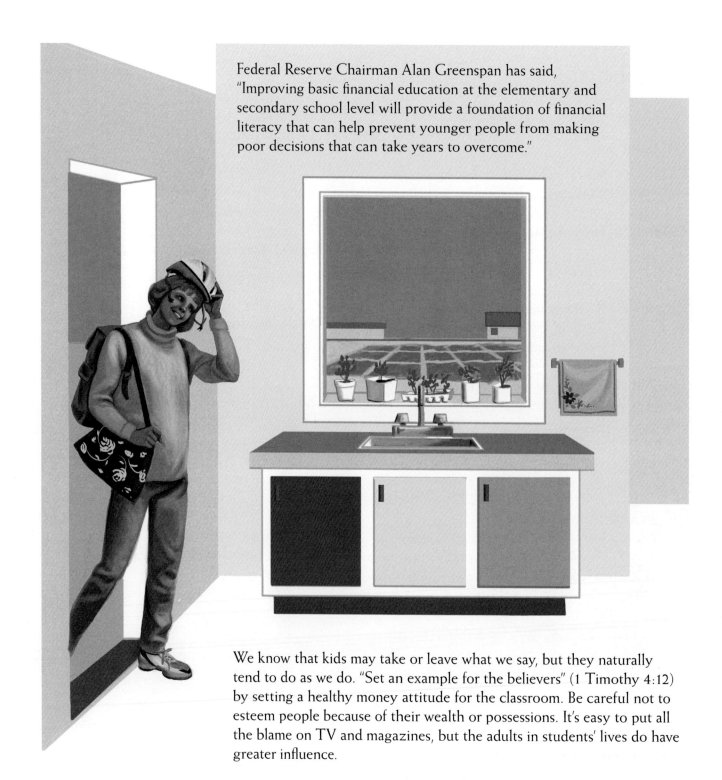

Federal Reserve Chairman Alan Greenspan has said, "Improving basic financial education at the elementary and secondary school level will provide a foundation of financial literacy that can help prevent younger people from making poor decisions that can take years to overcome."

We know that kids may take or leave what we say, but they naturally tend to do as we do. "Set an example for the believers" (1 Timothy 4:12) by setting a healthy money attitude for the classroom. Be careful not to esteem people because of their wealth or possessions. It's easy to put all the blame on TV and magazines, but the adults in students' lives do have greater influence.

Always encourage students to look for alternatives to buying stuff. For example, what do you do when the class calendar expires? Our first thought is to buy a new calendar. But what is really needed? A way to keep track of birthdays? A place where the lunch menu can be posted? What are some free ways to meet these needs? Even if you decide a new calendar is the best option, kids have learned creative problem solving.

As educators, we may be so glad to have an ambitious student we don't even question her motives. Remind students of the right reasons for studying and making good grades—to glorify God and learn more about His creation. The goal of "getting a job that pays lots of money" is not a good priority for any student in a Christian classroom.

Students can use the scripture index on pages 70-79 for a variety of activities—making posters, educating other classes, writing assignments, etc.

A Year of Good Stewardship

The 31st of **January** is Child Labor Day. Learn about exploitive child labor in North America and abroad through UNICEF or the National Consumers League Child Labor Coalition.

In Chapter 6, students study different types of love—romantic, brotherly, and "agape," God's self-sacrificing love. Discuss the different types of love in **February** on Valentine's Day.

On **March** 7th, 1933, the game Monopoly® was invented. Allow students to research real monopolies. Afterward, students can bring in a few boards from home, divide into groups, and play a round.

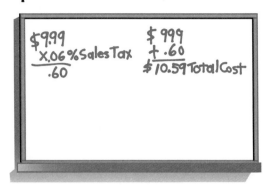

U.S. income taxes are due on **April** 15th. Use the opportunity to teach how taxes are collected and what they pay for. Do students know that even they pay sales tax? Advance classes can study "negative income tax," an idea that is popular among economists for helping the poor.

Celebrate **May** 20th, Good Neighbors Day, by sharing with students Jesus' definition of "neighbor" (Luke 10:29-37). Work together on a service-learning project to help neighbors around the world.

Have students observe Diary Month in **June** by keeping a daily record of how they spend money. Use these diaries to help students understand income and expenses, and develop a future budget.

Americans observe Independence Day on **July** 4th. Signed in 1776, the Declaration of Independence grants citizens the rights of "life, liberty, and pursuit of happiness." Often we confuse the pursuit of happiness with financial success. Ask students to think about other meanings.

During Clergy Appreciation Month in **October**, allow students to make cards to send to their pastors and study the tithing lessons in Chapter 1.

August is Family Fun Month and a great opportunity for students to take home what they're learning at school. Have students plan activities that don't involve "consuming," or spending money. They can take a walk with a grandparent, tutor a younger sibling, or ride bikes with a cousin.

The day after Thanksgiving is the biggest shopping day of the year. In **November**, help students plan an alternate way for the community to start the holiday season, such as reaching out to people in need.

The 21st of **September** is World Gratitude Day, a chance for students to be thankful for all of God's blessings, not just the store-bought ones.

In **December**, help students prepare for a Christmas that celebrates Jesus, not the toy and candy-cane industries. Sponsor a child as a class, suggest that students donate their favorite toys to a shelter, or think of homemade gifts to exchange.

Organizations and resources

Federal Reserve Education
www.federalreserveeducation.org

U.S. Department of the Treasury
www.ustreas.gov/education

U.S. Mint
www.usmint.gov/kids

Media Awareness Network
1500 Merivale Road
3rd floor
Ottawa, ON
K2E 6Z5
613-224-7721
info@media-awareness.ca
www.media-awareness.ca

Bank of Canada
www.bankofcanada.ca

Treasury Board of Canada
www.tbs-sct.gc.ca

Royal Canadian Mint
www.mint.ca

TV-Turnoff Network
1601 Connecticut Avenue NW
Suite 303
Washington, DC 20009
(202) 518-5556
email@tvturnoff.org
www.tvturnoff.org

Commercial Alert
4110 SE Hawthorne Blvd.
#123
Portland, OR 97214
(503) 235-8012
ingo@commercialalert.org
www.commercialalert.org

Recommended reading

Take Action! A Guide to Active Citizenship by Craig and Marc Kielburger: John Wiley & Sons, 2002. Step-by-step instructions for helping your students raise the standard of living for people in need at home and around the world.

Rich Christians in an Age of Hunger by Ronald J. Sider: Word Publishing, 1997. From the Midwest Book Review: Sider explains the complex causes of poverty, and presents practical, workable proposes for change, proposals that should be taken up by every man and every woman who seeks to deserve the title "Christian."

Kids as Customers by James U. McNeal: Lexington Books, 1992. This and other books about marketing to children are eye opening. Parents, teachers, and students themselves deserve to know strategies used for "Kid Kustomers."

Branded: The Buying and Selling of Teenagers by Alissa Quart: Perseus Publishing, 2003. Even though this book has "teenagers" in the title, the ideas are relevant to tweens and children. Quart reveals how kids are manipulated for profit through techniques such as "peer-to-peer marketing" and product placement in schools.

The Two-Income Trap: Why Middle-Class Mothers and Fathers Are Going Broke by Elizabeth Warren and Amelia Warren Tyagi: Basic Books, 2003. This ground-breaking book brings to light the surprising financial consequences of mothers going to work, and the precarious position of today's middle class. The authors contend, with carefully researched data, that contrary to popular myth, families aren't in trouble because they're squandering their second income on luxuries. They point to the ferocious bidding war for housing and education that has engulfed America's suburbs. Warren and Tyagi propose a set of innovative solutions, from rate caps on credit cards to open-access public schools, to restore security to the middle class.

Chapter 1—Nacho gold

"The silver is mine and the gold is mine," declares the Lord Almighty.

Haggai 2:8

We know that "the earth is the LORD'S, and everything in it" (Psalm 24:1), and the land beneath our feet is His, too (Leviticus 25:23)—even our bodies are not our own (1 Corinthians 6:19-20). But what about the Benjamins? Does it all belong to God—even Grandma's birthday money?

Teaching students that they are stewards of God's wealth is the first step in helping them to resist materialism. Instead of thinking "How can I make money?" or "How can I buy this?" they learn to ask "How can I use what I've been given for God's kingdom?" This may seem like an obvious question for any Christian, but it's a radical, revolutionary world view. Twenty-five hundred years since Haggai delivered his divine message, and the words still haven't lost their edge.

Did you know?

Students need to understand that being stewards is an important part of our identity as Christians—but it is just a part. As stewards we can fail, but we are first and foremost God's beloved children. Secure in this knowledge, we can see through the false "security" of money.

1 Chronicles 29:14 explains stewardship in a nutshell: "Everything comes from you [God], and we have given you only what comes from your hand."

Early Christians were familiar with the responsibilities of a steward—taking care of the master's household affairs. In 1 Corinthians 4:2 NKJV, we read ". . . it is required in stewards that one be found faithful." Are we supposed to judge our friends based on whether or not they are good stewards? Paul says no; only God has the right to judge our stewardship.

What's a steward?

The role of steward is an important part of any Christian's identity. Help students understand the concept of "stewardship" with this activity:

Begin by telling students that a steward is someone who takes care of another person's belongings. Assign one student volunteer the role of restaurant owner and ask her to name her restaurant (Taylor's Tacos, for example). She then must choose another student to be the restaurant manager. Explain that the manager will run the restaurant while the owner is working in her office in another city.

Have students suggest responsibilities the manager will have: making sure customers are satisfied with their food, money is deposited into the bank, employees get paid on time, the bathrooms are clean, etc. What qualities does the manager need? Students may suggest that the manager would have to be responsible, organized, and trustworthy. Taylor chooses James to be the manager. Emphasize that even though James is not the owner, he has to take care of Taylor's restaurant because he is the manager, or steward. Ask students these questions:

- Who owns Taylor's Tacos?

- Who is the manager, or steward, of the restaurant?

- What are other examples of stewards in everyday life? Who do you trust to take care of your stuff?

- Discuss the responsibilities of taking care of another's person's property. Ask students if any of them have jobs or responsibilities that make them stewards over another person's property such as dog walking or baby sitting.

Name_____

Stewardship in God's Word

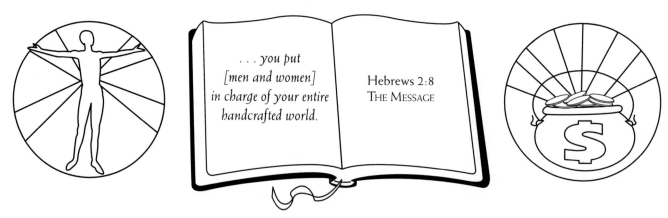

. . . *you put [men and women] in charge of your entire handcrafted world.*

Hebrews 2:8
THE MESSAGE

Answer the following questions.

1. Who put men and women in charge of the world?

    _____

2. Look up the following verses to find things that belong to God.

    Leviticus 25:23 _____

    1 Corinthians 6:19-20 _____

    Haggai 2:8 _____

3. What do we use today instead of gold and silver?

    _____

4. If our money belongs to God, how can we use it to glorify Him?

    _____

    _____

*Stewardship is what we do
after we say we believe.*

Empty your pockets!

Teach the basics of financial stewardship with this simple activity: Have students bring a few coins to class—pennies, nickels, dimes (the denomination does not matter). Put all the money in a tray or hat, and then ask students to figure out to whom each coin belongs. Impossible, they say?

Give students a Bible clue: Haggai 2:8. Talk about how everything is the Lord's and we are only stewards, or caretakers. This includes our pocket change, allowance, and all the stuff we buy with money, too, like toys and clothes. Now that students know money belongs to God, how might they treat it differently?

What about tithing?

What exactly is tithing? Is it the same thing as stewardship?

Begin this lesson by writing the word "tithe" on the board. Ask students to talk about what they think it means. Explain where the word itself came from: a tenth. Under the word "tithe," write "tenth" on the board for students to compare how similar they are. Have students say both words to hear how they sound similar.

Explain that on different occasions in the Bible, people gave a tenth, or 10%, of their belongings to God. For instance, if a family owned a flock of sheep that birthed 10 lambs, they would give one of the lambs to support the priests and temple.

Tithing in scripture

What was tithe used for in Bible times? Read Deuteronomy 14:22-29 as a class to find out:

> Be sure to set aside a tenth of all that your fields produce each year. Eat the tithe of your grain, new wine and oil, and the firstborn of your herds and flocks in the presence of the LORD your God at the place he will choose as a dwelling for his Name, so that you may learn to revere the LORD your God always.
>
> But if that place is too distant and you have been blessed by the LORD your God and cannot carry your tithe (because the place where the LORD will choose to put his Name is so far away), then exchange your tithe for silver, and take the silver with you and go to the place the LORD your God will choose. Use the silver to buy whatever you like: cattle, sheep, wine or other fermented drink, or anything you wish. Then you and your household shall eat there in the presence of the LORD your God and rejoice.
>
> And do not neglect the Levites living in your towns, for they have no allotment or inheritance of their own. At the end of every three years, bring all the tithes of that year's produce and store it in your towns, so that the Levites (who have no allotment or inheritance of their own) and the aliens, the fatherless and the widows who live in your towns may come and eat and be satisfied, and so that the LORD your God may bless you in all the work of your hands.

What's so special about the Levites? One of the twelve tribes of Israel, the Levites were set aside, or consecrated, by God to be priests. Because they weren't able to earn a living by farming, God commanded His people to tithe to the Levites and priests so that they could devote themselves to the Law (2 Chronicles 31:4).

Discussion questions

- Where were the Hebrews supposed to take their tithes? (to a far-off place God would choose "as a dwelling for His name")
- What were they supposed to do if they couldn't travel that far? (exchange the goods for silver and buy food or whatever they wanted)
- What did God tell them to do with their purchases? (feast with their families, rejoicing and celebrating God's blessings)
- Who did God tell them not to neglect? (the Levites, aliens (or foreigners), orphans, and widows living in their hometowns)
- What did God promise them if they obeyed His commands to tithe? (He would bless them in all the work of their hands).

Bonus: Have students look up Malachi 3:10 to find another of God's promises about tithing.

> "Bring the whole tithe into the storehouse, that there may be food in my house. Test me in this," says the LORD Almighty, "and see if I will not throw open the floodgates of heaven and pour out so much blessing that you will not have room enough for it."

For advanced classes, give students these scenarios and have them calculate the tithe:
Ten silver coins
Twenty jars of wine
Forty loaves of bread
Thirty fish
One hundred pieces of fruit

Tithing today

Today our tradition is to give 10% of our income (in the form of money, not grain or cattle!) to our church. Ask students to think about what the money is used for. Like the Levites, ministers today shouldn't have to have a second job to earn a living. Our tithes support them and their families. Tithes are often used for the day-to-day expenses of operating a church. Who pays for the yummy snacks you have on Wednesday night? The light bill? Even though churches don't make their members tithe or pay dues, they need the money to operate. In the Bible, the Jewish people paid an annual tax for the upkeep of the tabernacle and later the Temple in Jerusalem. Did Jesus and his disciples pay this tax? Have students read Matthew 17:27 to find out. God's commandments about tithing in the Old Testament can also teach us how to best use our tithes.

Discussion questions

- The ancient Hebrews gave their tithes to people in need—widows, orphans, and strangers. How can our churches do this today? (Community outreaches such as soup kitchens and children's homes)

- In the Bible, they used their tithes to celebrate God's blessings. Do we ever travel away from home and feast with our family? (Going to Grandma's for Thanksgiving, church suppers, etc.)

Name_____

Stewardship Crossword

Across

2. a tribe of Israel consecrated by God for priesthood
5. to set aside a tenth of what you make to honor God
6. a home

Down

1. foreigners or people traveling through the Israelites' towns
3. to take or give in return for something else
4. someone who takes care of another person's belongings

   CD-204009 *Taking Godly Care of My Money*

Chapter 2—Show me the . . . legal tender?

. . . money is the answer for everything.
Ecclesiastes 10:19

Is the writer of this passage, the wise and wealthy King Solomon, suggesting that money buys happiness?

Not likely—just a few chapters earlier he calls the pursuit of money "meaningless." Money, even though it's the source of so much worry and desire, is only good for things. In other words, money will not buy a ticket to heaven—but it will buy a ticket to the movies. For better or worse, it makes the world go 'round.

From the gold talents of King Solomon's time to today's credit cards, this chapter will help students see through the bling to understand money for what it is—a medium of exchange.

Did you know?

Alexis de Tocqueville, a Frenchman born 200 years ago, said "No stigma attaches to the love of money in America, and provided it does not exceed the bounds imposed by public order, it is held in honor. The American will describe as noble and estimable ambition that our medieval ancestors would have called base cupidity." Help students understand his words, and discuss if this judgment is still true today.

A good citizen should pay his taxes with a smile, but the government always insists on money!

Selected Literature

Neale S. Godfrey's Ultimate Kids Money Book by Neale S. Godfrey: Simon & Schuster Children's Publishing, 1998. From piggy banks to the Federal Reserve Bank, this cheerful approach to financial matters is fun and thorough.

Money: A History by Jonathan Williams: St. Martin Press, 1998. In our increasingly "cashless" society, this adult book's 500 illustrations, 200 of them in color, make a fine visual introduction to the history of money.

Oral tradition

One of the best-known stories in the Gospels about currency is Jesus' clever response to the question of paying tax to Rome. Help Mark 12:13-17 come alive by having students learn dramatic interpretation.

First read the story to students with little expression. Then read the story a second time with lots of expression. Does the story now seem to "come alive"? Explain to students how the Gospels were not written down until years after Jesus' life on Earth. In the meantime, the stories were memorized and spread by word of mouth—what we call oral tradition.

Ask students to interpret parts of Mark 12:13-17 by speaking with a specific tone of voice, emphasizing certain words, or adding body language and gestures. Help students think of ways to show certain feelings.

TV and movie actors have techniques to help the audience understand what's going on—for example, a character who is lying may avoid making eye contact or have nervous gestures like touching his mouth. Without thinking about it, we instantly understand the subtext, or the meaning that is not said out loud.

Family stories are a perfect example of oral tradition. Ask students for tales their grandparents enjoy sharing about their own childhood or Mom and Dad's. Have students tell a family story from memory and then write it down. How can they capture a mood in words? Are some feelings, such as irony or humor, harder to show?

Put each line of the dialogue on page 19 in context by reading the entire story, and having students take turns practicing the different moods.

This practice dialog on page 19 can serve as an audition or practice for the performance of the script that follows on pages 20 and 21.

Audition or practice for skit

1. Pharisee or Herodian: "Teacher, we know you are a man of integrity."
    Sincere—as if the Pharisee really means it
    Insincere—not telling the truth

2. Jesus: "Why are you trying to trap me?"
    Afraid—worried that they will trap him
    Angry—mad about their tricks
    Sad—disappointed in them
    Surprised—they had tried to match wits with Jesus earlier and he had put them in their place—why do they want to embarrass themselves further?

3. Jesus: "Whose portrait is this? And whose inscription?"
    Ignorant—as if he doesn't know the answer
    Confident—sure of himself

4. Pharisee or Herodian: "Caesar's."
    Sarcastic—like, duh!
    Impatient—annoyed, thinks Jesus is wasting their time

5. Jesus: "Give to Caesar what is Caesar's and to God what is God's."
    Humorous—winks at the crowd, gives everybody a laugh at the expense of the Pharisees and Herodians
    Serious—doesn't crack a smile

Which interpretations do students think are the most likely to have really happened?

Let students put it all together by practicing and performing the dramatic interpretation on pages 20-21.

Face Off!

Characters
Narrator
Jesus
Leader 1
Leader 2
Leader 3
Crowd member 1
Crowd member 2
Rest of the class:
members of the crowd

Props
One coin

Narrator: About two thousand years ago, in Jerusalem, people gathered to hear Jesus tell stories. One of his stories condemned powerful people—the Pharisees and Herodians. They wanted revenge . . . *(Narrator gestures toward group of religious leaders standing together off to the side).*

Leader 1: I've got it! We'll ask Jesus whether or not we should pay taxes to the emperor. If he says we should, he'll upset the zealots. If he says we shouldn't pay taxes to Caesar, Rome will execute him!

The leaders all laugh evilly.
Across the room, Jesus sits in the middle of a gathering of people. They are asking him questions about one of his parables.

Person 1 *(speaking in awe)*: Jesus, your story about the owner of the vineyard, are you the owner's son who they killed? Are you the "stone the builders rejected?"

Jesus starts to answer but **Person 2 interrupts**: Yeah! That's it! And you know who killed him? The Pharisees and Herodians! They are "the farmers" in Jesus' story. I hate those stupid Pharisees . . .

Meanwhile the leaders approach the crowd (unseen by Person 2) and stop to listen.

Person 2 *(continues)*: They think they're so special, prancing around in their fancy clothes *(mimics prancing)* . . . saying their long, boring prayers. "Almighty Lord, thank you for making me so rich and powerful and handsome *(makes an ugly face)* . . . blah, blah, blah . . ."

Leader 1: *clears his throat, and* **Person 2** *jumps around. The crowd laughs nervously.* **Person 2** *mumbles an apology and ducks behind Jesus for protection.*

Leader 1: *(with a big fake smile)*: Jesus, teacher, we are not insulted by your friend. We know that you are a man of integrity.

Leader 2: You aren't swayed by men, because you pay no attention to who they are. *(Gesturing to the crowd, under his breath)* And he must pay no attention to how they smell, either.

Leader 1: You teach the way of God in accordance with the truth.

The leaders look at one another excitedly, then say together: Is it right to pay taxes to Caesar . . . or not?

The crowd gasps and murmurs.

Person 1: What is Jesus going to say?

Jesus: Why are you trying to trap me?

The leaders look indignant, then start to squirm.

Jesus *(continues)*: Bring me a denarius and let me look at it.

Leader 1 gives Jesus the coin.

Jesus holds up the coin for everyone to see then flips it back to the Pharisee: Whose portrait is this? And whose inscription?

Leader 2 *fumbles the catch:* Where is this going? Of course it is a portrait of Caesar.

Jesus *(as if what he's saying should be obvious)*: Give to Caesar what is Caesar's and to God what is God's.

Jesus then turns and winks at the crowd.

They laugh, and the dumbfounded Pharisees hurry off with their mouths gaping open.

Worth a mint

Cash. Moolah. Bucks. Dough. It's all money, or currency. A way to exchange what you have for what you want.

Explain to students that before the bills and coins we have today, rare and precious resources such as gold and silver were used as currency. Why not dirt or water? The currency would be worthless, and everyone would soon be "rich"—rich as mud, that is.

Funny money

Instead of coins and bills, all kinds of different tokens have been used as money, and some people around the world continue to trade with traditional forms of currency:

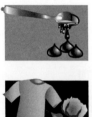 Aztecs: **chocolate**

 Nigerians: **strips of cotton cloth**

 Santa Cruz Islanders: **red feathers**

 Solomon Islanders: **dolphins' teeth**

 Ancient Romans: **lumps of salt**

 American Indians and early colonists: **clam shells**

 19th century Europeans: **grass clippings**

Find the counterfeit currency!
All of the above items have been used as currency except one. Ask students to guess the fake.

Answer: As far as we know, grass clippings were not used as currency in 19th century Europe.

An easier buck

Materials
  Scale
  1-, 2-, and 3-ounce bags of sand

Can students think of any reason gold, silver, or copper would be inconvenient currency? For one, it would have to be weighed every time you want to exchange it.

Have students practice with bags of sand. Ask them to pretend that it's gold dust—their new currency. Mark items in the classroom "for sale: 1 (or 2 or 3) ounce(s) of gold." Students must determine what they can afford to buy by weighing their bags on the scale.

Next, ask if students can think of a way to make the process easier. How about marking each bag with its weight?

Explain that coins are precious metals with their weight minted on them. Mints, the places where coins are made, have blanking machines that punch discs out of sheets of metal. Each disc is stamped with a design. The government determines how much each coin is worth—one cent, five cents, ten cents, etc. Pass change around class for students to study (include foreign coins, if possible, for variety).

Mark 12:13-17 also teaches us about currency in Jesus' time. The denarius features Caesar's portrait and inscription—and like our coins today, it was minted.

Bartering

Long gone are the days when you could trade your barrel of flour for a cow. If you want hamburgers, you have to buy them with dollars. Introduce the concept of bartering to students at lunchtime. Begin by explaining that people haven't always used bills and coins as money. For example, if a family had an apple orchard but no bread, they could trade with a baker—the family gets bread and the baker can make an apple pie.

Allow students to barter their lunches. If one student wants another student's dessert, what will it cost him? Is the brownie worth half a pizza? Remind students that they can use "goods" (like an apple) as well as "services" (offering to do something for someone, like put up his lunch tray). And if students don't strike a deal, that's okay, too—they only should buy or sell if both parties agree on a "fair price."

Bible barters

Have students look up the following references to see items that were bartered in Bible times.

Genesis 47:16
Because his brothers had no money, Joseph gave them food in exchange for their livestock.

Ezekiel 27:12-23
The people of Tyre have a thriving barter system. List at least nine goods they trade: (slaves, wheat, fine linen, honey, oil, cinnamon, lambs, goats, carpets)

1 Kings 5:10-11
Hiram, the king of Tyre, kept King Solomon supplied with all the cedar and pine logs he wanted, and in turn King Solomon gave Hiram years' worth of wheat and olive oil.

God's favor?

So far, we've learned about ancient exchange customs from the Bible. But what does Scripture tell us about money on a deeper level? Is wealth a worldly trap, or a sign of God's favor? People throughout history have drawn different conclusions to this question.

Sometimes we try to make the Bible fit our own opinion and desires. Help students become aware of their opinions with the *Opinion, Please* worksheet on page 26. Ask students to choose the person they think best fits each characteristic. Students don't need to justify their choice, but should just answer immediately with their gut reaction. Go down the list quickly, having students respond "A" or "B."

Afterward, discuss students' choices as a class. Are most of the positive words paired with the wealthy man, and negative words paired with the poor man? Why did students make these choices?

Explain to students that money doesn't make a person good or bad, important or unimportant. But comfort students by letting them know that people in Jesus' time made the same mistake. Have students read the following scripture:

As Jesus started on his way, a man ran up to him and fell on his knees before him. "Good teacher," he asked, "what must I do to inherit eternal life?" "Why do you call me good?" Jesus answered. "No one is good—except God alone. You know the commandments: 'Do not murder, do not commit adultery, do not steal, do not give false testimony, do not defraud, honor your father and mother.'" "Teacher," he declared, "all these I have kept since I was a boy." Jesus looked at him and loved him. "One thing you lack," he said. "Go, sell everything you have and give to the poor, and you will have treasure in heaven. Then come, follow me." At this the man's face fell. He went away sad, because he had great wealth. Jesus looked around and said to his disciples, "How hard it is for the rich to enter the kingdom of God!" The disciples were amazed at his words. But Jesus said again, "Children, how hard it is to enter the kingdom of God! It is easier for a camel to go through the eye of a needle than for a rich man to enter the kingdom of God."

Mark 10:17-25

The disciples were even more amazed, and said to each other, "Who then can be saved?"

The word "amazed" is translated from the Greek word *ekplesso*, meaning struck with panic, terrified, frightened, or "expelled by a blow." The disciples were blown away by Jesus' words!

Why were the disciples so shocked? Like many people today, they believed that wealth was a sign of God's approval and favor.

Most Christians today don't know much about John Calvin, but the 16th century Protestant reformer greatly influenced the way we think about wealth today. Puritans brought to the New World Calvinism's doctrine of predestination—the idea that a person's salvation was decided before birth. How could you tell if you were one of the select? Hard work, self-discipline, and success.

Can students see the danger in this line of thinking? When do we mistake God's mercy and patience for approval? For example, "God must not care too much that I lied to Sis because He hasn't interfered or let her find out."

Opinion, Please

Look at each word and choose the person you think best fits that characteristic. Write either A or B in the blank.

_____ Successful

_____ Dishonest

_____ Lazy

_____ Truthful

_____ Generous

_____ Kind

_____ Dangerous

_____ Trustworthy

_____ Happy

_____ Nice

_____ Important

_____ Unloved

_____ Friendly

_____ Content

_____ Nasty

_____ Smart

_____ Unloved

_____ Hero

_____ Loved

_____ Crook

_____ Blessed

Name _____

Show Me the Money

```
T  H  D  Y  O  Z  F  O  W  D  O  G  I  C  M  N  X  S  A  S  R  J  V  C  F
B  I  D  S  J  W  P  B  W  Y  W  N  K  N  U  I  O  Y  F  J  R  C  M  Z  J
D  R  A  L  U  A  R  O  I  X  S  I  I  U  V  R  I  N  I  J  T  Z  W  O  S
U  D  V  X  R  O  W  T  G  V  B  H  K  Y  F  C  R  W  X  Q  D  A  R  O  I
W  E  B  E  Z  T  Y  J  S  T  C  O  A  C  I  M  B  E  Y  V  D  Y  D  R  G
P  H  T  O  E  I  N  O  I  T  A  T  E  R  P  R  E  T  N  I  T  Z  G  A  R
C  O  F  F  P  I  W  D  X  S  U  B  X  V  F  E  R  W  A  C  K  Y  D  L  T
A  H  A  H  P  I  X  B  O  U  U  A  G  T  S  G  V  X  O  P  Y  W  G  T  A
C  J  I  J  O  F  H  A  A  C  F  S  Y  B  Y  P  Z  Q  N  T  F  Q  N  R  Z
I  H  R  A  O  V  J  W  R  D  K  M  W  R  G  T  X  R  D  S  N  W  R  A  S
V  V  P  O  C  V  O  H  T  N  Q  E  W  Y  E  O  D  Q  P  S  H  S  M  D  A
W  O  R  E  H  G  O  O  D  S  N  Q  G  R  G  T  P  X  M  F  S  G  X  I  A
E  U  I  A  F  G  T  D  N  N  Y  R  O  Z  Z  P  R  W  M  J  Y  H  M  T  C
Q  S  C  K  N  I  A  J  Y  S  K  L  G  K  A  J  O  A  K  S  Y  G  E  I  X
C  R  E  U  W  U  P  E  H  S  E  E  S  I  R  A  H  P  B  I  D  T  Y  O  H
J  H  Q  Y  O  G  E  J  K  U  P  L  Q  L  P  B  K  X  Q  U  J  S  K  N  Q
M  F  P  E  O  A  E  Q  I  X  H  S  D  H  O  P  Z  C  H  M  Z  G  G  H  F
```

Find these words in the puzzle above. Words can be found across, down, and diagonally.

WORD BANK

currency	money used to exchange things
barter	to exchange without money
interpretation	to explain the meaning of something
goods	products that people want or need
fair price	in economics, the price agreed upon by buyers and sellers
Pharisees	a group of Jewish leaders who believed in strict obedience to God's law
oral tradition	stories or beliefs handed down from generation to generation by word of mouth.

Chapter 3—It's the economy, students.

As goods increase, so do those who consume them. Ecclesiastes 5:11

Imagine this familiar scene at the grocery store: Mother and son have just started their trip down aisle one when Junior spies a green plastic thingamajig he really, really, really wants. Mom says no, son pleads as if his very life were on the line, and so it goes—thingamajig after thingamajig, for the entire shopping trip or till the end of time, whichever is over first.

Now, imagine this same scene after Junior has learned basic economic principles at school: "Mom, I really want the Bug Juice Sipper. But thinking in terms of cost-benefit theory, the 99-cent price tag does not include the energy I would have to expend to persuade you, or the expensive dental care a high-sugar diet requires. Our regular OJ will be just fine."

Or that's the goal, at least! By understanding our system of production and consumption, students can make more informed and ethical decisions.

Did you know?

Economics is not just about money—it's simply the study of choices. Ask students to think about the choices they've made so far today—when to get out of bed, what to wear, what to eat for breakfast, etc. All of the choices and decisions are examples of economics.

When's the last time students wanted something that they could not have? This experience is called scarcity. Everyone, poor and rich, has to go without certain things. Economics explains the choices we all make to cope with scarcity.

Among the economic observations King Solomon made in Ecclesiastes 5:10-20, he said, "As goods increase, so do those who consume them." What are goods? Who produces (or makes) them? Who consumes (or buys) the goods?

Selected Literature

Cost Benefit Jr.: How Free Markets Work by Stephanie Lynn Herman: Evergreen Colorado: Ah-Ha! Press, 2003. Microeconomic concepts are presented in a fun way kids can relate to and remember.

It's going to cost you

Ask students to define the word "cost," and they'll likely answer in terms of money, i.e. a soda costs a dollar. But do students know that cost is more than a price tag? The decisions we make are trade-offs—all our choices have costs and benefits.

Ask students to name the cost of sleeping late on a school day. The cost, or loss, could be upsetting your parents, not having time to eat breakfast, or being tardy. Next, discuss the benefit of sleeping late—you get to stay in your warm comfy bed and get a little more rest.

Is it more important to be on time or get extra sleep? The answer can vary from person to person, from day to day. If you're really sleepy, you might choose the benefit of staying in bed. If you have an important test first thing in the morning and you can't be late, you'll probably choose the benefit of being on time.

Opportunity cost

Whatever we choose to do, we could have done something else instead. We do our first choice, and the next best choice is the "opportunity cost." On a typical school night, students can choose to watch TV, walk the dog, hang out with friends, play on the computer, do chores, finish homework, etc.—but they don't have time to do it all.

Ask students to write down what they were doing last night at seven o'clock. What would they have been doing if they had not chosen this activity? This next best choice is the opportunity cost. For example, Emil's favorite TV show might come on at seven, but his soccer practice is at the same time. The opportunity cost of the TV show for Emil is missing soccer practice.

How much?

Go over the following situations as a class and have students name their own opportunity cost, or next best choice:

1. Going to church on Wednesday nights
    Sample responses:
    Miss baseball practice
    Don't get to chat with my friends on the computer

2. Attending school
    Sample responses:
    Don't get to sleep really late
    Can't play all day

3. Spending allowance on soda
    Sample responses:
    I'd want to save up for a guitar instead
    Rather go to the movies

Now that students have determined the cost of each choice, go back and have them name the benefits. For example, what are the advantages of going to school? Responses may include learning, hanging out with friends, and avoiding punishment from parents.

In each situation, when does the benefit outweigh the cost? For instance, students are present at school because the benefit of attending outweighs the cost of not getting to sleep late or not being able to play all day.

For the third situation, each student will probably have a different idea for how they would spend their money. Something has "utility" if it meets your wants or needs. Ask students to name products that have utility for them. Talk about how something that has utility for one person can be worthless for someone else.

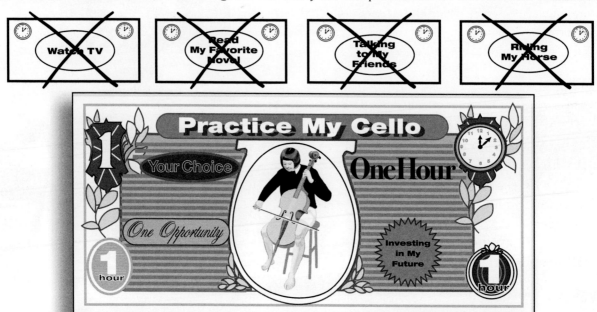

What's it worth to you?

Economics assumes that people make decisions based on their own self-interest, an idea called "rational choice theory." In other words, we try to make choices that give us the most benefit at the least cost.

For a long time social scientists believed that religious decisions were irrational, or not based in self-interest. But economists are beginning to realize that when we help others, we also help ourselves. Discuss with students—what are the costs of being a Christian, and what are the benefits?

Some Romans thought the early Christians were crazy—why help the poor or sick? What could they do for you? But because they nursed the sick, Christians received nursing. Because they aided the less fortunate, they received aid when they needed it. They loved others and were in turn loved. Discuss 2 Corinthians 8:14 with students: "Your plenty will supply what they need, so that in turn their plenty will supply what you need. Then there will be equality."

Cost-benefit analysis

Have each student think of an activity he would like to try, such as taking swimming lessons, getting a new pet, or learning a foreign language. Then, have children complete the *Cost-Benefit Analysis* worksheet on page 32 to see if the activity is worth doing. Here's a sample:

Activity: Learning to play the guitar

   Costs

1. Have to spend lots of time practicing, wouldn't get to watch as much TV.
2. Would need a guitar, would have to be extra nice to brother so he lets me borrow his.
3. Lessons are $20 a week, would have to do extra chores and use all my allowance (couldn't buy any video games).

Students would choose the cost, or negative incentive, that's most important to them.

   Benefits

1. Get to perform at the talent show in front of an audience.
2. Can learn to play my favorite songs.
3. Other people will admire me; I could even be famous.

Students would choose the benefit, or positive incentive, that's most important to them.

Which is greater, the costs or the benefits? Is the activity worth trying?

Name _____

Cost-Benefit Analysis

Choose an activity to analyze:

Activity _____

List 3 Costs of this activity.

1. _____

2. _____

3. _____

Circle the number of the cost, or negative incentive, that's most important to you.

List 3 Benefits of this activity.

1. _____

2. _____

3. _____

Circle the number of the benefit, or positive incentive, that's most important to you.

Which is greater, the costs or the benefits? Is the activity worth trying?

_____

_____

Ask your parents if they can think of any more costs or benefits you might not have considered.

_____

_____

_____

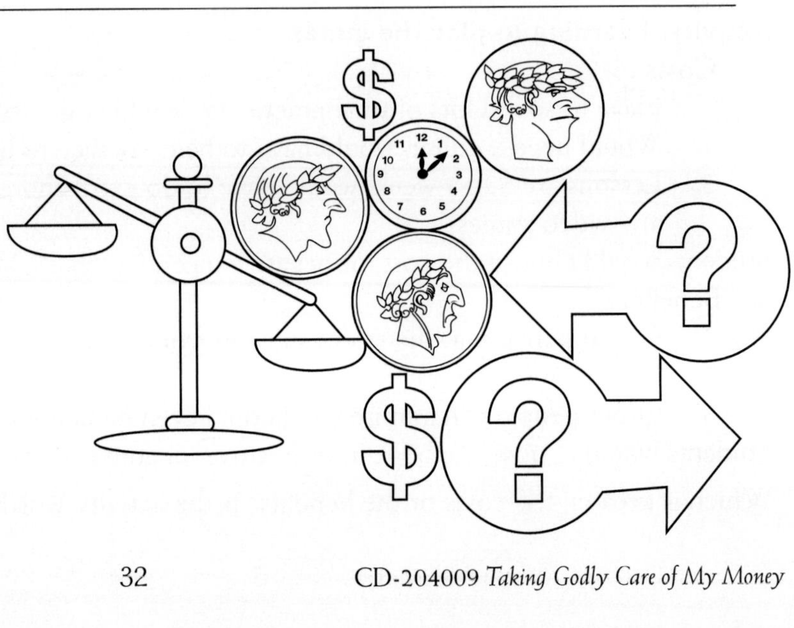

Incentives

Benefits and costs are incentives—a motivation for behavior. Before doing anything, we think about our incentives. Students are already familiar with incentives if your classroom has reward charts, and here are some more examples to go over as a class:

<u>HUNGER</u> is an incentive to eat.

_____ is an incentive to do well in school.

_____ is an incentive to brush your teeth.

_____ is an incentive to eat junk food.

_____ is an incentive to eat healthy foods.

_____ is an incentive to shoplift.

_____ is an incentive not to shoplift.

_____ is an incentive to spend your allowance today.

_____ is an incentive to save for the future.

_____ is an incentive to lie about losing your friend's CD.

_____ is an incentive to tell the truth about losing your friend's CD.

_____ is an incentive to give money to charity.*

_____ is an incentive to honor your parents.**

* Have students look up Proverbs 19:17 to find this incentive.

** Have students look up Exodus 20:12 to find this incentive.

CD-204009 *Taking Godly Care of My Money*

Macroeconomics

So far, the ideas in this chapter have focused on microeconomics, or the study of individual choices. Macroeconomics is the big picture—the study of governments' choices. Governments can support three different types of markets: free markets, controlled markets, and mixed markets.

Free Market

Most economists agree that free markets, in which scarcities are resolved through changes in prices, raise the standard of living for everybody. Milton Friedman, the Nobel-prize winning economist, claims the free market system is the most ethical system of exchange because of its mutually-beneficial, non-coercive nature.

Materials:

Candy for each student plus one extra piece

Demonstrate a free market to students by telling them you have a bag of candy at home. You will bring it in tomorrow to sell to each student who wants a piece. Hold up one piece of candy to show students what they're buying. Decide on a "fair price"—the term economists use to describe what the buyers are willing to pay and what the seller is willing to accept. Write the amount on the board.

Next, inform students that today you have one piece of candy, which you will sell to the highest bidder. Only the person who gives you the most money will get the candy. Do you hear 5 cents? 10? 25? The highest bid will most likely well exceed the price agreed upon earlier.

Why do students think they are willing to pay more for the same piece of candy? Can students think of other examples of scarcity raising the price of goods? Why are popcorn and soda more expensive at the movies than they are at the grocery store?

Controlled and mixed markets

In a controlled market, government regulations determine the price of goods. In a mixed market, some goods are regulated and some are not.

Supply and demand worksheet

In the previous activity, students who wanted to buy the candy expressed "demand." The teacher provided the "supply." Have students match the supplies and demands on page 35.

         CD-204009 *Taking Godly Care of My Money*

Name _____

Supply and Demand

Draw a line to match the *supply* on the left with the *demand* on the right.

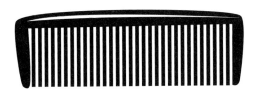

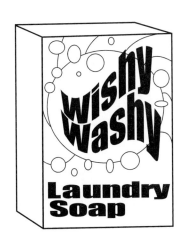

CD-204009 *Taking Godly Care of My Money*

Name_____

Economically Speaking

Match the word to its correct definition.

1. _____ Consumption
2. _____ Microeconomics
3. _____ Scarcity
4. _____ Cost
5. _____ Goods
6. _____ Production
7. _____ Benefit
8. _____ Opportunity Cost
9. _____ Economics
10. _____ Macroeconomics
11. _____ Free market

A. products that people want or need

B. work that has value to others

C. to spend or use goods

D. the study of choices

E. the study of individuals' choices

F. the study of government choices and the global economy

G. shortage

H. a price or loss

I. an advantage or gain

J. The next-best option sacrificed when we make a choice

K. system of production and consumption in which scarcity is resolved through price changes, not regulation

Who was the first businessman?

Noah
While all the rest of the world
went into liquidation,
he floated his own company!

CD-204009 *Taking Godly Care of My Money*

Chapter 4—But I want an Oompa Loompa now!

Give everyone what you owe him: If you owe taxes, pay taxes; if revenue, then revenue; if respect, then respect;
if honor, then honor. Let no debt remain outstanding, except the continuing debt to love one another,
for he who loves his fellowman has fulfilled the law.
Romans 13:7-8

It only takes a few minutes of channel surfing to realize that many adults are overwhelmed with financial pressures. Commercial after commercial promises viewers a way out of debt, each preceded and followed by an advertisement for the latest pill, antiperspirant, or frozen pizza.

Even a small allowance or pocket change allows students to develop budgeting skills that will last a lifetime. The lessons in this chapter will focus on earning, tithing, saving, investing, and spending wisely.

Did you know?

Students can't yet take out car loans or mortgages, but they can still get into bad habits of wanting more and more. School-age children are ready to learn delayed gratification and contentment.

Kids may not deal with large sums of money, but they can still be stewards over the "few things" they do have:

"His master replied, 'Well done, good and faithful servant! You have been faithful with a few things; I will put you in charge of many things. Come and share your master's happiness!'"
Matthew 25:21

What is debt?

Unfortunately, all too many students are probably familiar with the idea of debt. If they haven't overheard their parents arguing about bills, they've seen the credit card ads and bankruptcy commercials. Share this simple definition of debt with students: something owed. What are some examples of debt? If students have ever asked for an advance on their allowance, they know the feeling of being in debt. They still have to do their chores, but the money's already been spent!

CD-204009 *Taking Godly Care of My Money*

Debt or "credit?"

Creditors, or lenders, know that people don't like the word "debt." Instead, they use something that sounds nicer: "credit." Instead of a debt card, it's a "credit" card.

Familiarize students with a useful word: euphemism—substituting a less direct word for a blunt or distasteful word. With the following examples, say the "offensive" word and have students give the more common euphemism. Which ones are meant to be polite? Do any cover up something bad or wrong? Are there some that are just supposed to be funny?

She smells bad. (*Is odorously challenged*)

Something I ate gave me diarrhea. (*Montezuma's revenge, runny tummy, etc.*)

In 1949, the United States Department of War changed its name to the Department of ? (*Defense*)

Chew your food thoroughly or you'll fart. (*Pass gas, cut the cheese, etc.*)

My best friend is crippled. (*Disabled, physically challenged*)

Be careful eating peanut brittle if you wear false teeth. (*Dentures*)

The Nazis used the euphemism, Final Solution, to hide their mass murder of Jewish people. (*The Holocaust*)

Hobos hang out on that street. (*Homeless people*)

The war caused 500 casualties. (*Deaths or serious injuries*)

There are a lot of old people in my neighborhood. (*Senior citizens*)

He lies. (*Fibs, is thrifty with the truth*)

Excuse me, where is the toilet? (*powder room, rest room, bathroom*)

According to bathroom historian Frank Muir, ancient Israelites called their facilities the "House of Honor."

Class budget

Because students' situations are different with allowances and spending money, create a classroom budget. Ask each student to contribute a small amount, say fifty cents, every week to the class budget. Mark four shoeboxes—"giving," "long-term savings," and "short-term spending." Let the class decide what percentage to allocate each jar. For instance, if the class collects 40 quarters each week, they may decide to give 15 of them away through charity and tithes, keep 10 for long-term savings goals, and put 5 toward short-term spending.

It's important that students determine how to use the money. First, ask students to decide to whom they would like to receive their "giving" money (see pages 66-67 for ideas). Next, have students suggest big items to save for such as a class pet, sports equipment, or computer game. Make sure students understand what's realistic by helping them estimate costs and remember hidden expenses (i.e. cage, food, water bottle, toys, shavings, and veterinary care for the "free" rabbit).

Finally, decide what will be left over for short-term spending goals. This could be enough for a special snack each month or a new favorite book for the class library. It's important that the budget not be set in stone, and that students are allowed to learn from their mistakes. Review it with students at least once a month to reevaluate revenue and expenses.

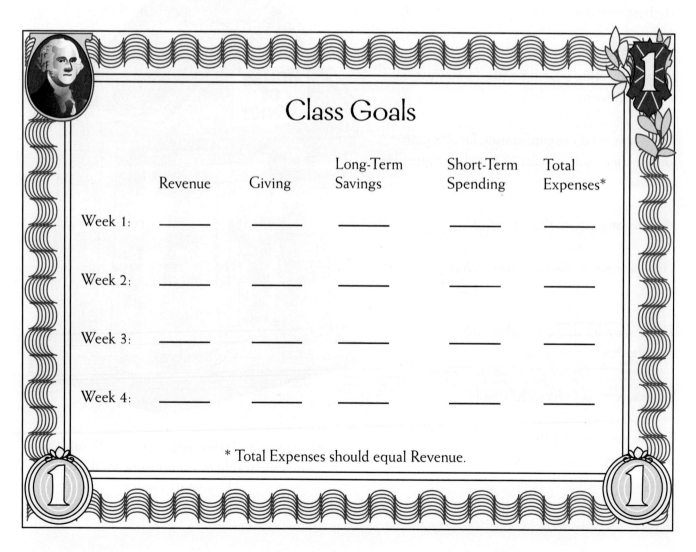

Class Goals

	Revenue	Giving	Long-Term Savings	Short-Term Spending	Total Expenses*
Week 1:	_____	_____	_____	_____	_____
Week 2:	_____	_____	_____	_____	_____
Week 3:	_____	_____	_____	_____	_____
Week 4:	_____	_____	_____	_____	_____

* Total Expenses should equal Revenue.

Repo man!

Lenders today may hound delinquent customers, but it's nothing new. Ask a student to read Proverbs 22:26-27:

Do not be a man who strikes hands in pledge or puts up security for debts;
if you lack the means to pay, your very bed will be snatched from under you.

Explain to students how borrowing works in the adult world. If you want a new bike that costs $249.99, but you don't have the money in the bank to pay for it, you can charge it to a credit card. Cool, huh? Why don't we all go out and buy ourselves some new bikes?

$249.99

MISS A PAYMENT, LOSE THE BIKE!

Unfortunately, the loan has some strings attached. You must pay the credit card company back within 30 days, or they charge you interest, or a fee for borrowing money. For example, you let a friend borrow five bucks—in a week she has to give you the five dollars back, plus fifty cents. Fifty cents is the interest charge.

A common credit card interest rate currently is 18.99%, or $47.47 for a $249.99 bike if paid off in one year. And on top of that, the credit card company can take your bike back if you miss a payment—just what King Solomon warned about in his proverb.

$$\begin{array}{r} \$249.99 \\ +\ 47.47 \\ \hline 297.46 \end{array}$$

The magic of compound interest

Do students know there's a way to sit back and watch your bank account grow (or shrink), without having to lift a finger? It's called compound interest, and here's how it works.

Remember the $249.99 bike that ended up costing $297.46? If you make only small monthly payments, or skip payments as credit card companies often allow, the bike will end up costing even more than that—hundreds or even thousands of dollars.

Ask students to imagine . . . their hard-earned money has to go toward paying for a bike (and the interest on it) that they already have. Even if the tire is busted and they can't ride it, even if they leave it on the street and somebody steals it. And if Grandma sends $50 in a birthday card—exactly what they need for the video game they've been wanting? Too bad, the money has to go toward the stupid bike they had to have that they don't even like that much anymore.

Demonstrate the concept of compound interest to students with the following exercise.

Law requires credit card companies to require minimum monthly payment of at least 2.5% or $10, whichever is higher.

Bike's original cost in the store: $249.99

Interest rate (or APR) Annual Percentage Rate: 18.99%

If you make the minimum payment of $10 each month, it would take over 41 months to pay off the bike. That's almost three and a half years!

Interest charges would add $160.10 to the cost of the bike, which would end up costing 410.09!

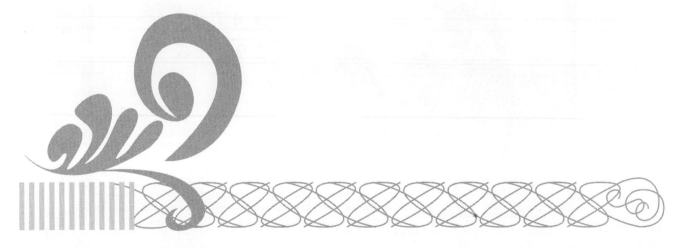

Interest in the Bible

The Bible contains warnings against making money by lending money—a practice that is almost a way of life in our society. The word "usury" has almost slipped from our vocabulary. Explain to students that usury means charging interest on loans. Have children study scriptures on the subject with the *Economically Speaking* worksheet on page 44.

Help students understand "profit" by asking how much one of their belongings cost (a $30 backpack, for example). Explain that if you pay them $30, they don't make any money. If you pay them $40, however, they make a $10 profit.

Usury in history

For hundreds of years after Jesus' time, the Church forbade usury, or charging interest. But as Europe approached the Renaissance in the 12th and 13th centuries, trade increased. The emerging merchant class required a system of lending. Because guilds and other skilled occupations were closed to Jews, the job of loaning money fell to them. Christians considered themselves superior to Jewish people, and they soon began to resent their debt to them. There were common outbreaks of violence against the Jewish community.

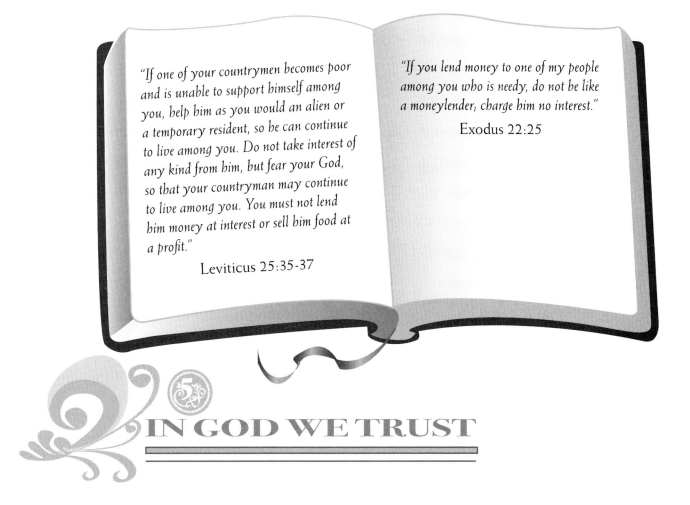

"If one of your countrymen becomes poor and is unable to support himself among you, help him as you would an alien or a temporary resident, so he can continue to live among you. Do not take interest of any kind from him, but fear your God, so that your countryman may continue to live among you. You must not lend him money at interest or sell him food at a profit."

Leviticus 25:35-37

"If you lend money to one of my people among you who is needy, do not be like a moneylender; charge him no interest."

Exodus 22:25

IN GOD WE TRUST

Name _____

Economically Speaking

Read the Bible verses below to answer the questions.

1. Today, the point of most businesses is to make money, or a profit. God tells the Israelites to NOT profit off a countryman who becomes

_____.

2. Why do you think God had Moses forbid Israelites from charging their brothers, or neighbors, interest?

_____

_____

3. Why do you think it was okay to lend to strangers and foreigners with interest?

_____

_____

4. Today, banks only lend to people who they believe will pay them back. They make sure the borrower has a good job and has always paid his bills on time. Who does Jesus say we should lend to?

_____

_____

5. What crimes do we think of as detestable, or really terrible? Why do you think lending at usury and taking too much interest was considered so hateful?

_____

_____

"If you lend money to one of my people among you who is needy, do not be like a moneylender; charge him no interest." Exodus 22:25

LORD, who may dwell in your sanctuary? Who may live on your holy hill? He . . . who lends his money without usury.
Psalm 15:1-5

He does detestable things. He lends at usury and takes excessive interest. Will such a man live? He will not!
Ezekiel 18:12-13

"And if you lend to those from whom you expect repayment, what credit is that to you? Even 'sinners' lend to 'sinners,' expecting to be repaid in full. But love your enemies, do good to them, and lend to them without expecting to get anything back. Then your reward will be great, and you will be sons of the Most High, because he is kind to the ungrateful and wicked. Be merciful, just as your Father is merciful."
Luke 6:34-36

Spending wisely

In our consumer culture, the dollars we spend have a big influence. Even children have "buying power." Let students in on some exciting news—even before they turn eighteen, they can "vote!" They may not be able to choose the president, but their pocket change can "vote" in other ways.

For example, ask students to think of a type of food they wish their favorite restaurant would add to its menu. If the restaurant gets enough people interested in the same item, they'll offer it. In that way, students "vote" for the food by buying it.

What's fair

Explain to students that there are more serious ways to "vote" with their money. In Chapter 3, students learned how economists define "fair"—a fair price is one on which the buyer and seller both agree. "Fair" is used in another way, too. "Fair trade" means more equitable, less exploitive dealings with producers in developing countries. Share this concept to students with the following demonstration:

Attach a paper wrapper from two chocolate bars. Label one "Fair Trade, $1.00" and the other "Fair Price 75¢." (Review the definition of "fair price" from page 34 if necessary.) Inform students that these two candy bars are for sale. They look and taste the same, but there is one difference: the one marked "fair price" is like any other candy bar you see in the grocery store. The price is called "fair" because the manufacturer and you, the buyer, agreed on it. You "agreed" when you decided to buy it at the store.

The chocolate marked "fair trade" is a little different. For one, why does it cost more? Begin by explaining how fair trade works: The people who grow the cocoa beans to make the chocolate are paid more. Instead of giving their employees the very minimum (say $2-3 dollars for a full day of work), the candy maker pays them enough so that they can afford a home, food, and school for their children. The customer—whoever buys the chocolate at the store—pays extra so that workers in poor parts of the world earn more. Fair trade buyers also work against child slavery and other unethical labor practices.

Which chocolate do students want to buy? How much more are they willing to pay for the fair trade chocolate? Ten cents? Fifty cents? More? What are they getting in exchange for the higher cost?

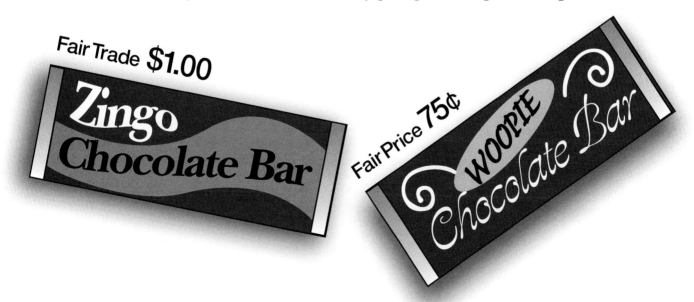

Fair Trade

Using a world map or globe, point out the West African nations, such as the Ivory Coast, Ghana, Nigeria, and Cameroon where most of the world's supply of cocoa is grown. Fair Trade products are gaining in popularity. Ask students to be on the lookout for certified chocolate as well as other items such as fruit, sugar, coffee, tea, rice, and even sports balls.

Look for this symbol that signifies a fairly-traded product. Students can learn more about fair trade at:

www.fairtradefederation.com
www.transfairusa.org

Name _____

Fair Scales

Farmers in poor parts of the world are often taken advantage of by buyers who use inaccurate and dishonest weights. Unscramble the vocabulary words below. Then solve the coded puzzle to find out the blessing of using fair scales.

1. something owed   B T E D   _ _ _ _ _

2. the ability to borrow, sometimes used instead of "debt"   I R T E D C   _ _ _ _ _ _
                                                                                                        2   12

3. substituting a less direct word for a more blunt word   I E M M S H U P E   _ _ _ _ _ _ _ _ _
                                                                                                              7

4. money received when selling something   V N E E U R E   _ _ _ _ _ _ _
                                                                                                          13   6

5. a type of savings for future needs   O G L N - M R T E   _ _ _ _-_ _ _ _
                                                                              11   14 5

6. costs   P N E E S X S E   _ _ _ _ _ _ _ _
                                                                                        9 10

7. a fee charged by a moneylender   E S I T T R E N   _ _ _ _ _ _ _ _
                                                                                          4

8. interest   R U S Y U   _ _ _ _ _

9. a plan for expenses   T G B U E D   _ _ _ _ _ _
                                                                              3

10. a type of interest earned or paid on interest   P D N C M O O U   _ _ _ _ _ _ _ _
                                                                              8

11. more equitable, less exploitive dealings with producers in developing countries.   A I R F   D R T A E   _ _ _ _   _ _ _ _ _
                                                                                                              1

YOU MUST HAVE _ _ _ _ _ _ _ _
              1 2 2 3 4 1 5 6

AND _ _ _ _ _ _ WEIGHTS AND
    7 8 9 6 10 5

MEASURES, SO THAT YOU MAY

_ _ _ _ _ _ _ _ IN THE LAND
11 12 13 6 11 8 9 14

THE LORD YOUR GOD IS GIVING YOU. DEUTERONOMY 25:15

Chapter 5—On guard!

"Watch out! Be on your guard against all kinds of greed; a man's life does not consist in the abundance of his possessions."

Luke 12:15

Long before a 4.2 million square-foot mall sprang up in the middle of America, Jesus spoke of the dangers of materialism. More than a few people in the audience were poor and hungry, and many probably considered themselves blessed to have a second set of clothes. None of them had a cell phone or four-wheel drive; very few worked 40-plus hour weeks—and Jesus warned them against greed!

Even kids' possessions are becoming more abundant (Barbie and Ken need cell phones, too!). Students have commercials coming at them from every direction—from internet pop-up ads to their friend's new sneakers that might as well be called Air Covet. The activities in the following chapter will help them learn to "watch out!"

Did you know?

Greed, or wanting more and more, is treated by most of us as one of the more "minor" sins, like telling a white lie. But in Colossians 3:5, Paul calls it "idolatry." Discuss with students how greed is like worshiping an idol.

What does Jesus mean by "all kinds of greed?" Is it possible to be greedy whether you have a lot or a little? When we think about what would make us happy, we tend to focus on money and possessions. Ask students to name other blessings, from health and family to bear hugs and summer vacation.

Who Touched the Remote Control: Television and Christian Choices by Mary Duckert: Friendship Press, 1990. Focuses on how teachers and parents can help students become critical viewers and make Scripture-based decisions about television.

Kids Talk TV: Inside Out by Cade Bursell and Carol Tizzano: United Church of Christ Office of Communication, 1996. Games and activities to teach children how to respond to the media messages they receive everyday.

But Me That! Consumers Union, 1990. The toys (and hairstyles) in this video may be out-of-date, but the information is as relevant as ever. Kids will learn to develop a healthy skepticism at the advertising targeted at them.

Wish list

We're all familiar with feelings of greed, even if we don't call it that. As a class, make a wish list—things students would buy if they won a shopping spree—cell phones, the latest computer games, go-carts, etc.

Encourage them to include every single last item they can think of. When they're done, make it clear that there shouldn't be one more thing they want. Take a final look at the list, and ask students how they would feel if they did have everything they named. Satisfied?

The next week ask students if there's anything they'd like to add to the list. Draw a line under the first list and add their new requests; repeat each week for a month or so.

Once the original list has grown to include more and more things, share this simple definition of greed with students: being eager to have more. Discuss why it's easy to feel we'll be happy if only we have this or that. Why is there always one more thing we want? Why did Jesus tell us to watch out for this?

Explain to students that it's not that God doesn't want us to have fun—he just knows that toys and other possessions won't bring lasting happiness. Only by trusting in Him can our hearts and minds be truly satisfied.

The previous activity seems to suggest that kids are materialistic and toy-grubbing —but of course this could not be further from the truth. It is, after all, grown ups who are responsible for kids' consumer appetites. Adults target children with sophisticated advertising and marketing ploys, and parents pony up the cash. Children, so sensitive to people hurting or in need, will almost always choose helping another over their own gain. We adults are responsible for nurturing this behavior.

It keeps going, and going, and going . . .

Why does God want us to depend on Him, and not stuff? For one, He's forever, and our stuff isn't. How many times have students longed after a certain toy with all their hearts, only to get tired of it? Read John 4:13-14 with the class:

> *Jesus answered, "Everyone who drinks this water will be thirsty again, but whoever drinks the water I give him will never thirst. Indeed, the water I give him will become in him a spring of water welling up to eternal life." The woman said to him, "Sir, give me this water so that I won't get thirsty and have to keep coming here to draw water."*

As a class, discuss how our belongings are like the water in this story. They satisfy us for a little while, but soon we want more. Jesus offers us something that never wears out, or gets boring, or gets replaced with a newer model.

> *Do not wear yourself out to get rich; have the wisdom to show restraint. Cast but a glance at riches, and they are gone, for they will surely sprout wings and fly off to the sky like an eagle.* Proverbs 23:4-5

The word "rich" comes from the Hebrew word *ashar*, which also means "to pretend to be rich." Aspiring to the standard of living we see on TV takes a lot of hard work and money, too!

The eight or nine commandments

We like to think of ourselves as a society whose law is rooted in Judeo-Christian law, especially the Ten Commandments. Ask students to name as many commandments as they can. Unless they've recently memorized them for class, they'll likely remember them in order of "importance," or how our culture ranks them. The commandments against killing, committing adultery, and stealing are well-known, and we remind children frequently to honor their fathers and mothers. But what about coveting, or keeping the Sabbath? Breaking these commandments is ingrained in our culture. Certain commandments we go so far as to abbreviate—for example, leaving off how God tells us to keep the Sabbath holy.

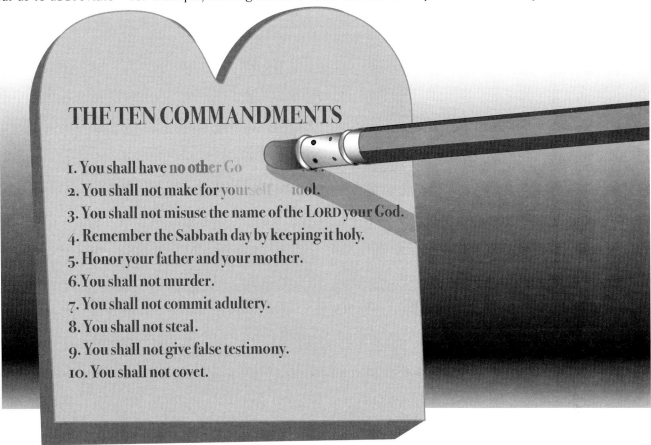

THE TEN COMMANDMENTS

1. You shall have no other Go............
2. You shall not make for yourself .... idol.
3. You shall not misuse the name of the LORD your God.
4. Remember the Sabbath day by keeping it holy.
5. Honor your father and your mother.
6. You shall not murder.
7. You shall not commit adultery.
8. You shall not steal.
9. You shall not give false testimony.
10. You shall not covet.

Illustrate this point with a story about the imaginary "Kali-kali people of Little Backwards Island." Explain to students that their society is very different from ours: one day each week, everyone rests. They prepare ahead of time so that no one has to work or cook or wash or go anywhere on that day. While we may eat out after church on Sunday, their restaurants are closed on their "Sabbath." It's a crime just to put burgers on the grill for dinner!

Another strange thing about these people is their law about wanting more than you have. If you work really hard in school so that you can get a good job and make lots of money—they put you in jail! If your friend is wearing new shoes that you really like, it's against the law to want a pair for yourself. Is that weird or what? And you know who doesn't go to jail? Murderers! For the Kali-kali people, it's perfectly okay to offer human sacrifices on altars for giant gold idols!

Now, ask students to guess the religion of the Kali-kali people. Are they pagans or heathens? No—they're Christians. "How can that be?" students may ask. Point out how the Kali-kali people do follow some commandments, and ignore others. They don't covet or work on the Sabbath, but they do kill and worship idols. If this sounds bizarre, have students think about which of God's laws we think are important, and which ones we take less seriously.

Covet

The word covet has almost slipped from our vocabulary. Help students realize its importance by discussing the tenth commandment:

You shall not covet your neighbor's house. You shall not covet your neighbor's wife, or his manservant or maidservant, his ox or donkey, or anything that belongs to your neighbor. Exodus 20:17

Explain to students that "to covet" simply means "to desire or wish for." Today most people don't have servants, oxen, or donkeys. What are other things our neighbors and friends have that we may covet? Is it possible to covet things we see on TV?

He who dies with the most toys . . . loses!

Sometimes we want more and more in order to feel secure. Ask students for examples of possessions that tend to make people feel safe, such as a house, food, and clothes. Sometimes things we don't even really need—like a certain brand of shoes—make us feel better about ourselves. Soon we begin to rely on things instead of God.

Read Luke 12:15-21 (NKJV) as a class:

And [Jesus] said to them, "Take heed and beware of covetousness, for one's life does not consist in the abundance of the things he possesses." Then He spoke a parable to them, saying: "The ground of a certain rich man yielded plentifully. And he thought within himself, saying, 'What shall I do, since I have no room to store my crops?' "So he said, 'I will do this: I will pull down my barns and build greater, and there I will store all my crops and my goods. And I will say to my soul, "Soul, you have many goods laid up for many years; take your ease; eat, drink, and be merry." ' "But God said to him, 'You fool! This night your soul will be required of you; then whose will those things be which you have provided?' "So is he who lays up treasure for himself, and is not rich toward God."

Name _____

Parable of the Rich Fool

Read Luke 12:15-21 and answer the questions.

1. What did the rich man do with his extra crops?

    _____

    _____

2. Why did he store his crops and goods in big barns?

    _____

    _____

3. How did the rich man think he would feel after "retiring?"

    _____

    _____

4. What kinds of "barns" do we have today, for storing our things and money?

    _____

    _____

5. We usually think of saving for the future as a good thing. When does it become as bad thing?

    _____

    _____

Where your heart is

Divide Luke 12:29-34 between nine students. Have students memorize and perform their lines with expression, one after another, in front of the class:

1. "And do not set your heart on what you will eat or drink; do not worry about it.
2. For the pagan world runs after all such things, and your Father knows that you need them.
3. But seek his kingdom, and these things will be given to you as well.
4. Do not be afraid, little flock, for your Father has been pleased to give you the kingdom.
5. Sell your possessions and give to the poor.
6. Provide purses for yourselves that will not wear out,
7. a treasure in heaven that will not be exhausted,
8. where no thief comes near and no moth destroys.
9. For where your treasure is, there your heart will be also."

We talk about a person's heart "being in the right place." Where does Jesus say our hearts are? Have students think of places we put our treasures, and write them on the board. Where are some better places to give our money or put our treasure?

Treasure boxes

Allow children to make these treasure boxes to use for giving needs, or for the budgeting activity on page 40. Decorate the shoeboxes as "treasure chests."

Materials
4 shoeboxes
Tempera paint
Brushes
Duct tape
Flat-back, colorful rhinestones
Glue

Instructions
1. Paint the box and lid the same color; let paint dry.
2. Using a different color, paint straps and lock.
3. Paint the keyhole in detail.
4. Attach the lid with duct tape (put the tape at the back, on the inside of the box).
5. Decorate with a few rhinestones.
6. Label the box "giving," "long-term saving," or "short term spending." Display the boxes under a banner that reads "For where your treasure is, there your heart will be also."

Slogans

Advertisers rely on our coveting their products. As a class, collect slogans that try to appeal to our desire for more, or tell us that we'll be happier or better in some way if we buy what they're selling. Encourage students to add a new slogan to the list everyday. Discuss each slogan as a class—why is it catchy or memorable? What does it promise?

Have it your way!
Don't Dream It, Drive It, Eye It, Try It, Buy It.
Bet You Can't Eat Just One.
The Happiest Place On Earth
We Love to See You Smile.
Breakfast of Champions

The abundant life

In Luke 12:15, Jesus warns against abundant possessions, but in John 10:10 NKJV, He uses the word "abundant" in a positive way: "I have come that they may have life, and that they may have it more abundantly." Explain to students that "abundant" comes from a Latin word that means "to overflow," or to have more than enough. What do students think it means to have life "more abundantly"?

X-rated

If "Lifestyles of the Rich and Famous" represented the excess and materialism of the 80s, greed is just hitting its stride today. Ask students to name TV shows that glamorize wealth and possessions, or lure contestants and viewers with millions in prize money. Must subjects endure humiliation or deceive others to win? Write their answers on the board.

Then discuss which of these shows have restricted ratings (such as TV-MA, mature audiences only). Even though they glorify avarice and covetousness, most of them are considered suitable for children. Let the class create a new rating: "TV-X" for excessive greed. Let the class decide which programs deserve this rating, and keep a list in class.

It's good to be ... what?

One popular show that certainly deserves a TV-X rating is *It's Good to Be ... A Cash Course on the Lifestyles of the Filthy Rich and Famous* on E!. Each episode features a celebrity and his or her expensive toys. Record and share a clip with the class, and ask students which celebrities have been featured recently. Why does the show choose these people? List answers on the board:

> *They're rich.*
> *They own lots of stuff.*
> *They have pushy or outrageous personalities.*
> *They do shocking things.*
> *They have good publicists.*

Now, inform students that they're going to create their own version of the show. (page 57 worksheet) Each member of the class is going to choose someone to write about in their report "It's good to be _____." But instead of choosing their subjects based on wealth, students will choose them based on who Jesus said it's good to be—in the Beatitudes.

Explain to students that the word "blessed" means "happy." Ask them to describe what makes them happy, and then read Matthew 5:3-10.

Encourage students to choose someone who we don't usually consider especially blessed, or "having it all" like pop stars and other celebrities. Is there a teacher at the school who is known for being modest or humble? Who is known for his peacemaking efforts? Do students know someone who has lost a friend or family member?

Just because we don't notice greed doesn't mean it's not there.
Remind students that the more common something is, like air, the easier it is to forget about. Students should think about these questions in their reports:

1. Why would your subject not be featured on the program "It's Good to Be . . ."?

2. Does Jesus say your subject is blessed? Why?

3. What can others learn from this person?

         CD-204009 *Taking Godly Care of My Money*

Name _____

Blessed Are . . .

Read each beatitude and write the name of a person who it reminds you of.

_____ Blessed are the poor in spirit, for theirs is the kingdom of heaven.

_____ Blessed are those who mourn, for they will be comforted.

_____ Blessed are the meek, for they will inherit the earth.

_____ Blessed are those who hunger and thirst for righteousness, for they will be filled.

_____ Blessed are the merciful, for they will be shown mercy.

_____ Blessed are the pure in heart, for they will see God.

_____ Blessed are the peacemakers, for they will be called sons of God.

_____ Blessed are those who are persecuted because of righteousness, for theirs is the kingdom of heaven.

Choose one person to write about.

It's good to be_____ because . . .

_____

_____

_____

_____

_____

_____

_____

Daily Loaded

Blessed be the Lord, Who daily loads us with benefits. Psalm 68:19 NKJV

Read the comic strip and then answer the questions.

"SON, AT THIS RATE, WE WON'T HAVE A FIRE UNTIL NEXT WINTER. I THOUGHT YOU WANTED TO ROAST MARSHMALLOWS TONIGHT!"

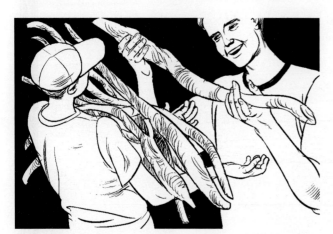

"HERE, HOLD OUT YOUR ARMS AND LET ME LOAD YOU UP!"

"THANKS, DAD! YOU HELPED ME GET TWICE AS MUCH WOOD IN HALF THE TIME!"

Is working really hard for what we want always the best answer? Why or why not?

_____

_____

What's the difference between going after riches yourself, and being "loaded" with them?

_____

_____

Daily breakfast burrito

Kids (and adults) sometimes pray as if Santa is on the other end of the line. The people in Jesus' time surely had long lists of wants and needs, too, but Jesus told them only to ask for their day's bread:

"This, then, is how you should pray: 'Our Father in heaven, hallowed be your name, your kingdom come, your will be done on earth as it is in heaven. Give us today our daily bread. Forgive us our debts, as we also have forgiven our debtors. . . . "

Matthew 6:9-12

Point out to students how the only thing Jesus tells us to ask for is our daily bread. What about butter and jam? Or clothes to wear? Jesus' audience may have asked him the same question, because right afterward He answers our question. Read Jesus' answer for the class, acting out the bold-faced words for the class to guess.

Matthew 6:24-33

*"You cannot serve both God and **Money**. Therefore I tell you, do not worry about your life, what you will **eat** or **drink**; or about your **body**, what you will **wear**. Is not life more important than **food**, and the body more important than **clothes**? Look at the **birds** of the air; they do not sow or reap or store away in barns, and yet your heavenly Father **feeds** them. Are you not much more valuable than they? Who of you by worrying can add a single hour to his life?*

*"And why do you worry about **clothes**? See how the lilies of the field grow. They do not **labor** or spin. Yet I tell you that not even Solomon in all his splendor was dressed like one of these. If that is how God clothes the grass of the field, which is here today and tomorrow is thrown into the fire, will he not much more clothe you, O you of little faith? So do not worry, saying, 'What shall we **eat**?' or 'What shall we **drink**?' or 'What shall we **wear**?' For the pagans run after all these things, and your heavenly Father knows that you need them. But seek **first** his kingdom and his righteousness, and all these things will be **given** to you as well."*

Name _____

Vocabulary Crossword

Across

3. wanting wealth or possessions more than helping others
5. a catch phrase used in advertising
6. wanting more

Down

1. belongings, stuff you buy
2. happy
4. over and above, or more than enough

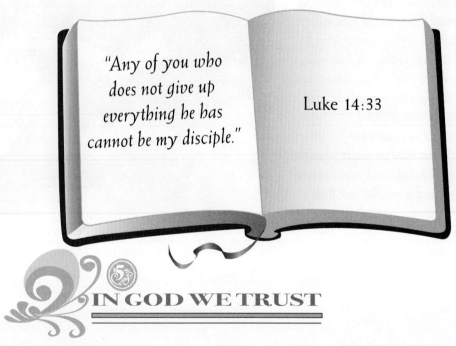

"Any of you who does not give up everything he has cannot be my disciple."

Luke 14:33

IN GOD WE TRUST

Chapter 6—Jesus Claus ain't coming to town?

"By . . . hard work we must help the weak, remembering the words the Lord Jesus himself said:
'It is more blessed to give than to receive.'"

Acts 20:35

"It is more blessed to give than to receive." We try to impart this wisdom to children every December—but it's hard to sound convincing. Who among us lives as if it's true? We'd all prefer Jesus and Santa working in cahoots, making our Christmas dreams come true year-round.

But Jesus taught again and again on the importance of helping the poor. Not once did he mention saving for college. Learning to give "freely and wholeheartedly" (1 Chronicles 29:9) is the most important financial lesson we can teach students—everything else is just details.

Did you know?

We'd prefer to be charitable only when we have extra to spare, but the chapter verse reveals something important about giving—it's not easy. Hard work and sacrifice are necessary.

This is how we've come to understand and experience love: Christ sacrificed his life for us.
This is why we ought to live sacrificially for our fellow believers, and not just be out for ourselves.
If you see some brother or sister in need and have the means to do something about it
but turn a cold shoulder and do nothing, what happens to God's love? It disappears. And you made it disappear.
My dear children, let's not just talk about love; let's practice real love.
This is the only way we'll know we're living truly, living in God's reality.
1 John 3:16-19 THE MESSAGE

Beyond tithing

Which is worth more—a penny or a dollar? If students have been paying any attention at all in school, they'll be quick to answer "a dollar." Complete the following lesson to show students how Jesus flipped this "right" answer right on its head!

In the first chapter, students learned how God instructed the ancient Israelites to give a tenth of their harvests. But Jesus demands even more of His followers. In Mark Chapter 12:38-44, Jesus condemns the wealthy synagogue leaders with their fine clothes and high social standing, even though they give big offerings to the temple. These men are like the most popular kids at school: greeted by everyone in the market (or hallway), and seated in the best places at banquets (or the cafeteria).

Instead of esteeming these powerful men like everyone else does, Jesus points to a woman, a poor widow. She's probably hungry and dressed in rags, but she puts all the money she has into the "offering plate," or temple treasury. It's only two small coins, worth less than a penny, but Jesus esteems her gift above the gold of the wealthy men:

Calling his disciples to him, Jesus said, "I tell you the truth, this poor widow has put more into the treasury than all the others. They all gave out of their wealth; but she, out of her poverty, put in everything—all she had to live on." Mark 12:43-44

Discuss Jesus' words with students. Why is her penny "more" than all the big donations? What percentage of her money did the widow give away—a tenth, half, or everything? How is the widow's action different from the Israelites' tithes in the Old Testament?

Charity

Charity—now that's a word we don't hear too much anymore. And when we do, it often has a negative connotation. No one wants to be a "charity case."

Help students understand the positive meaning of the word by having them look it up in the dictionary. Write the various definitions on the board (you may wish to paraphrase): giving to the poor, mercy in judging others, God's compassion for people, brotherly love.

How did the word for "love" come to mean helping those in need? Provide the class with the King James Version of 1 Corinthians 13.

Students are probably used to reading the word "love" here instead of "charity." Explain to students that when the King James Version of the Bible was translated in 1611, the word "charity" meant a specific kind of love. It means something different from the love you feel toward your mom or dad or your best friend. The word charity meant "self-sacrificing love" or "God's love." What does "charity" mean today? Why do students think the definition has changed over time? How are "giving to the poor" and "God's love" related?

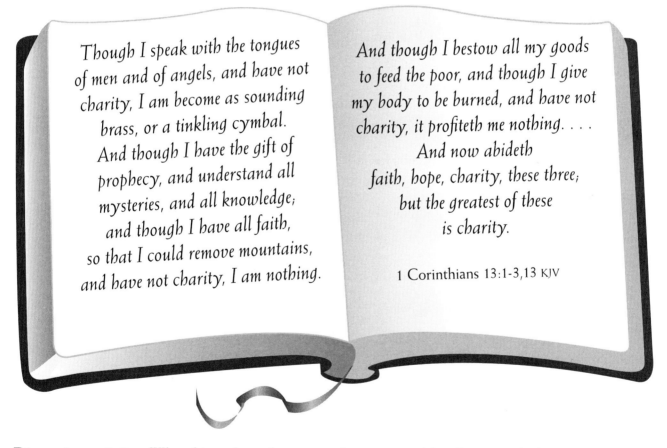

Though I speak with the tongues of men and of angels, and have not charity, I am become as sounding brass, or a tinkling cymbal. And though I have the gift of prophecy, and understand all mysteries, and all knowledge; and though I have all faith, so that I could remove mountains, and have not charity, I am nothing.

And though I bestow all my goods to feed the poor, and though I give my body to be burned, and have not charity, it profiteth me nothing. . . . And now abideth faith, hope, charity, these three; but the greatest of these is charity.

1 Corinthians 13:1-3,13 KJV

Discussion activity: What things do we have more than one word for? For example, how many different words can students think of that mean friend? Even though "buddy," "pal," "amigo," and "best friend" mean roughly the same thing, there are small differences. Ask students to describe how a "buddy" is different from a "best friend?"

Skit

First Corinthians 13, the "Love Chapter" has more to tell us about the relationship between helping the poor and "self-sacrificing love." The two are not the same:

And though I bestow all my goods to feed the poor . . . and have not love, it profits me nothing.

1 Corinthians 13:3 NKJV

Discuss with students how you can give without God's love by giving reluctantly or grudgingly. Illustrate this point with the following skit. Afterward, talk about cheerful giving.

The Grace to Give

Setting: Church service

Characters: Mom, Dad, their daughter, minister, and an usher

Props: An offering plate, daughter has money, bills or coins

Daughter sits between Mom and Dad. All three listen to the Minister.

Minister: Today we will be collecting offerings to help build a Christian school in Ethiopia.

Daughter looks down at the money in her hand and quickly puts it in her pocket.

Mom: Do you not want to help the children in Ethiopia?

Daughter: Yes, I mean no. I need this money to give Carrie, so she will make me a necklace.

Dad: Which is more important—the necklace or the children in Africa?

Daughter: *(mumbling)* The children . . .

Usher hands the plate to Mom who holds it in front of the daughter. Looking upset, the daughter slowly gets the money from her pocket and puts it in the plate.

Let each one [give] as he has made up his own mind and purposed in his heart,
not reluctantly or sorrowfully or under compulsion, for God loves
(He takes pleasure in, prizes above other things, and is unwilling to abandon or to do without)
a cheerful (joyous, "prompt to do it") giver [whose heart is in his giving].

2 Corinthians 9:7 THE AMPLIFIED

Don't put words in God's mouth

What does the Bible have to say about how we should treat our money and our belongings? Not always what we'd expect! Go over these questions with the class, having students try to figure out which words are God's. The correct answers are in bold-faced type.

1. Give to everyone who:
   a. **Asks you** *(Matthew 5:42)*
   b. Is your brother in Christ
   c. Obeys the Law

2. God loves a _____ giver.
   a. Generous
   b. Wealthy
   c. **Cheerful** *(2 Corinthians 9:7)*

3. He who gives to the poor:
   a. **Lends to the Lord**
      (Proverbs 19:17)
   b. God loves him more
   c. Will soon be poor himself

4. The man with two [coats] should:
   a. Wear them both at once so as not to catch cold
   b. **Share with him who has none** *(Luke 3:11)*
   c. Sell one, and use the money to buy food for his family

NEW! Introducing the **Erasable Bible**

Get rid of those objectionable passages!

5. _____, and it will be given to you.
   a. Love the Lord your God
   b. Don't sin
   c. **Give** *(Luke 6:38)*

6. Sell your possessions and give to: .
   a. The Believers
   b. **The poor** *(Luke 12:33)*
   c. Caesar

7. No one can serve two masters. Either he will hate the one and love the other, or he will be devoted to the one and despise the other. You cannot serve both God and: .
   a. Satan
   b. Your parents
   c. **Money** *(Matthew 6:24)*

8. Jesus looked at [the rich young man] and loved him. "One thing you lack," he said. "Go, sell _____ and give to the poor, and you will have treasure in heaven."
   a. Half your belongings
   b. **Everything you have** *(Mark 10:21)*
   c. Candy to babies

Where to start

In Chapter 4, students learned how to develop and follow a budget. Now that students have begun setting aside money in their "giving" treasure chest, help them decide what to do with it. Here are some places to start:

Partner with a less privileged school—www.donorschoose.com allows donors to fund a specific class project in a school where almost every student qualifies for free lunch. Students can choose from teacher-submitted proposals, such as helping East Harlem third-graders see *Beauty and the Beast* on Broadway, or buying uniforms for a girl's basketball team in rural North Carolina.

Is there a children's home in your area? Help children investigate the facility's needs and determine a fund-raising goal.

Adopt grandparents at a nursing home or senior center. Students could use their savings to buy a garden bench, repair a piano, or plan a group picnic.

Charities

Meals on Wheels serves millions of elderly, disabled, and at-risk people through home-delivered and congregate meal programs.
Meals on Wheels
1414 Prince Street
Suite 302
Alexandria, Virginia 22314
(703) 548-5558
www.mowaa.org

Africare gives students an opportunity to learn about and help one of the neediest parts of the world.
Africare
Africare House
440 R Street, N.W.
Washington, DC 20001-1935
(202) 462-3614
www.africare.org

Camp AmeriKids, an AmeriCares program, provides a traditional camping experience for children living with HIV/AIDS. Students can send a kid to camp, or donate items like disposable cameras, flash lights, and bathing suits to the camp wish list.

Camp AmeriKids
88 Hamilton Ave.
Stamford, CT 06902
(800) 486-4357
www.campamerikids.org

Catholic Relief Services is a great resource for teachers and students who want to reach out to suffering people in North America and abroad. Their site for children has puzzles, games, fast facts, and a kid-friendly newsroom.

Catholic Relief Services
209 West Fayette Street
Baltimore, MD 21201-3443
(800) 736-3467
www.catholicrelief.org/kids

Mercy Corps International offers classroom tools for teachers and students to learn about regions challenged by war and famine.

Mercy Corps International
(800) 292-3355
www.mercycorps.org

Church World Service, a ministry of thirty-six Protestant, Orthodox, and Anglican denominations, provides relief, development, and refugee assistance in the U.S. and overseas.

Church World Service
28606 Phillips Street
P.O. Box 968
Elkhart, IN 46515
www.churchworldservice.org
(800) 297-1516

Fund raising

Do students want to give more to charity than their class budget allows? Put the fun in fund raising with these money-making activities:

Students can continue the lesson in Chapter 4 by selling items that are certified Free Trade, such as chocolates and coffee. The sale can also serve as a "teach-in" to educate others about Free Trade.

Host a walk-a-thon. Students can organize pledges from individuals and businesses. Try to make tie-ins to your charity—for example, if you're raising donations for AmeriKids, have a summer camp theme. Or learn a recipe for a popular snack in the region you're helping and sell it at the event.

Perform the *Face Off* skit (page 20), or the *Grace to Give* skit (page 64) before an audience and charge admission. Have students write and stage two or three more scripts that illustrate giving grudgingly versus giving cheerfully.

If students are raising money to fight hunger, have them solicit local restaurants to donate a raffle prize of dinner for two.

Outline a map of the world on the gym floor, and have students organize a penny drive to fill each continent.

Organize a Dress-Down Day. Students may pay a small fee to dress outside the school's code.

Study the culture of a needy region, and have students create related artwork (i.e. recreations of traditional crafts). Host an exhibition or auction to raise money for that part of the world.

To Sum It All Up . . .

Did you know the entire Bible can be summed up in just five words? To find out, unscramble each word and then match the corresponding letters to complete the Bible verse.

1. I A Y T R H C .... giving to the poor, love, God's compassion for people

___ ___ ___ ___ ___ ___ ___
    11 6   4

2. R H U C F E L E ...... happy, in a good mood

___ ___ ___ ___ ___ ___ ___ ___
10   3   13 1

3. I V E G .... to put in the possession of another for his use

___ ___ ___ ___
  2

4. G I U N D G G R .... unwilling, reluctant, or sparingly

___ ___ ___ ___ ___ ___ ___
   5   9   7

5. C I I F E A C S R ..... to give up something

___ ___ ___ ___ ___ ___ ___ ___
12   8

The entire law is summed up in a single command:

" ___ O ___ ___   ___ O ___ ___   ___ ___ ___ ___ ___ B O ___
  1   2 3   4   5 6   7 3 8 9 10   6

___ ___   ___ O ___ ___ ___ ___ ___ ___."
11 12   4   5 6 12 3 1 13

Galatians 5:14

SCRIPTURE INDEX
Chapter 1—Nacho gold

Theme verse

"The silver is mine and the gold is mine," declares the LORD Almighty.
Haggai 2:8

Chapter verses

. . . the earth is the LORD'S and everything in it. Psalm 24:1

"The land must not be sold permanently, because the land is mine and you are but aliens and my tenants." Leviticus 25:23

Do you not know that your body is a temple of the Holy Spirit, who is in you, whom you have received from God? You are not your own; you were bought at a price. Therefore honor God with your body. 1 Corinthians 6:19-20

"Everything comes from you [God], and we have given you only what comes from your hand." 1 Chronicles 29:14

"It is required in stewards that one be found faithful." 1 Corinthians 4:2 NKJV

. . . you put [men and women] in charge of your entire handcrafted world. Hebrews 2:8 THE MESSAGE

Be sure to set aside a tenth of all that your fields produce each year. Eat the tithe of your grain, new wine and oil, and the firstborn of your herds and flocks in the presence of the LORD your God at the place he will choose as a dwelling for his Name, so that you may learn to revere the LORD your God always. But if that place is too distant and you have been blessed by the LORD your God and cannot carry your tithe (because the place where the LORD will choose to put his Name is so far away), then exchange your tithe for silver, and take the silver with you and go to the place the LORD your God will choose. Use the silver to buy whatever you like: cattle, sheep, wine or other fermented drink, or anything you wish. Then you and your household shall eat there in the presence of the LORD your God and rejoice. And do not neglect the Levites living in your towns, for they have no allotment or inheritance of their own. At the end of every three years, bring all the tithes of that year's produce and store it in your towns, so that the Levites (who have no allotment or inheritance of their own) and the aliens, the fatherless and the widows who live in your towns may come and eat and be satisfied, and so that the LORD your God may bless you in all the work of your hands. Deuteronomy 14:22-29

"Bring the whole tithe into the storehouse, that there may be food in my house. Test me in this," says the LORD Almighty, "and see if I will not throw open the floodgates of heaven and pour out so much blessing that you will not have room enough for it." Malachi 3:10

He ordered the people living in Jerusalem to give the portion due the priests and Levites so they could devote themselves to the Law of the LORD. 2 Chronicles 31:4

"Then the sons are exempt," Jesus said to him. "But so that we may not offend them, go to the lake and throw out your line. Take the first fish you catch; open its mouth and you will find a four-drachma coin. Take it and give it to them for my tax and yours." Matthew 17:27

Chapter 2—Show me the . . . legal tender?

Theme verse

. . .money is the answer for everything.
Ecclesiastes 10:19

Chapter verses

Later they sent some of the Pharisees and Herodians to Jesus to catch him in his words. They came to him and said, "Teacher, we know you are a man of integrity. You aren't swayed by men, because you pay no attention to who they are; but you teach the way of God in accordance with the truth. Is it right to pay taxes to Caesar or not? Should we pay or shouldn't we?"

But Jesus knew their hypocrisy. "Why are you trying to trap me?" he asked. "Bring me a denarius and let me look at it." They brought the coin, and he asked them, "Whose portrait is this? And whose inscription?"

"Caesar's," they replied.

Then Jesus said to them, "Give to Caesar what is Caesar's and to God what is God's."

And they were amazed at him. Mark 12:13-17

"Then bring your livestock," said Joseph. "I will sell you food in exchange for your livestock, since your money is gone." Genesis 47:16

" 'Tarshish did business with you because of your great wealth of goods; they exchanged silver, iron, tin and lead for your merchandise. " 'Greece, Tubal and Meshech traded with you; they exchanged slaves and articles of bronze for your wares. " 'Men of Beth Togarmah exchanged work horses, war horses and mules for your merchandise. " 'The men of Rhodes traded with you, and many coastlands were your customers; they paid you with ivory tusks and ebony. " 'Aram did business with you because of your many products; they exchanged turquoise, purple fabric, embroidered work, fine linen, coral and rubies for your merchandise. " 'Judah and Israel traded with you; they exchanged wheat from Minnith and confections, honey, oil and balm for your wares. " 'Damascus, because of your many products and great wealth of goods, did business with you in wine from Helbon and wool from Zahar. " 'Danites and Greeks from Uzal bought your merchandise; they exchanged wrought iron, cassia and calamus for your wares. " 'Dedan traded in saddle blankets with you. " 'Arabia and all the princes of Kedar were your customers; they did business with you in lambs, rams and goats. " 'The merchants of Sheba and Raamah traded with you; for your merchandise they exchanged the finest of all kinds of spices and precious stones, and gold. " 'Haran, Canneh and Eden and merchants of Sheba, Asshur and Kilmad traded with you. Ezekiel 27:12-23

In this way Hiram kept Solomon supplied with all the cedar and pine logs he wanted, and Solomon gave Hiram twenty thousand cors of wheat as food for his household, in addition to twenty thousand baths, of pressed olive oil. Solomon continued to do this for Hiram year after year. 1 Kings 5:10-11

As Jesus started on his way, a man ran up to him and fell on his knees before him. "Good teacher," he asked, "what must I do to inherit eternal life?" "Why do you call me good?" Jesus answered. "No one is good—except God alone. You know the commandments: 'Do not murder, do not commit adultery, do not steal, do not give false testimony, do not defraud, honor your father and mother.'"

"Teacher," he declared, "all these I have kept since I was a boy."

Jesus looked at him and loved him. "One thing you lack," he said. "Go, sell everything you have and give to the poor, and you will have treasure in heaven. Then come, follow me."

At this the man's face fell. He went away sad, because he had great wealth. Jesus looked around and said to his disciples, "How hard it is for the rich to enter the kingdom of God!"

The disciples were amazed at his words. But Jesus said again, "Children, how hard it is to enter the kingdom of God! It is easier for a camel to go through the eye of a needle than for a rich man to enter the kingdom of God." Mark 10:17-25

Chapter 3—It's the economy, students.

Theme verse

As goods increase, so do those who consume them.
Ecclesiastes 5:11

Chapter verses

Whoever loves money never has money enough; whoever loves wealth is never satisfied with his income. This too is meaningless. As goods increase, so do those who consume them. And what benefit are they to the owner except to feast his eyes on them? The sleep of a laborer is sweet, whether he eats little or much, but the abundance of a rich man permits him no sleep. I have seen a grievous evil under the sun: wealth hoarded to the harm of its owner, or wealth lost through some misfortune, so that when he has a son there is nothing left for him. Naked a man comes from his mother's womb, and as he comes, so he departs. He takes nothing from his labor that he can carry in his hand. This too is a grievous evil: As a man comes, so he departs, and what does he gain, since he toils for the wind? All his days he eats in darkness, with great frustration, affliction and anger. Then I realized that it is good and proper for a man to eat and drink, and to find satisfaction in his toilsome labor under the sun during the few days of life God has given him-for this is his lot. Moreover, when God gives any man wealth and possessions, and enables him to enjoy them, to accept his lot and be happy in his work-this is a gift of God. He seldom reflects on the days of his life, because God keeps him occupied with gladness of heart. Ecclesiastes 5:10-20

Your plenty will supply what they need, so that in turn their plenty will supply what you need. Then there will be equality. 2 Corinthians 8:14

He who is kind to the poor lends to the LORD, and he will reward him for what he has done. Proverbs 19:17

"Honor your father and your mother, so that you may live long in the land the LORD your God is giving you. Exodus 20:12

Chapter 4—But I want an Oompa Loompa now!

Theme verse

Give everyone what you owe him: If you owe taxes, pay taxes; if revenue, then revenue; if respect, then respect;
if honor, then honor. Let no debt remain outstanding, except the continuing debt to love one another,
for he who loves his fellowman has fulfilled the law.
Romans 13:7-8

Chapter verses

"His master replied, 'Well done, good and faithful servant! You have been faithful with a few things; I will put you in charge of many things. Come and share your master's happiness!'" Matthew 25:21

Do not be a man who strikes hands in pledge or puts up security for debts; if you lack the means to pay, your very bed will be snatched from under you. Proverbs 22:26-27

"If one of your countrymen becomes poor and is unable to support himself among you, help him as you would an alien or a temporary resident, so he can continue to live among you. Do not take interest of any kind from him, but fear your God, so that your countryman may continue to live among you. You must not lend him money at interest or sell him food at a profit." Leviticus 25:35-37

"If you lend money to one of my people among you who is needy, do not be like a moneylender; charge him no interest." Exodus 22:25

Lord, who may dwell in your sanctuary? Who may live on your holy hill? He ...who lends his money without usury. Psalm 15:1-5

He does detestable things. He lends at usury and takes excessive interest. Will such a man live? He will not! Ezekiel 18:12-13

"And if you lend to those from whom you expect repayment, what credit is that to you? Even 'sinners' lend to 'sinners,' expecting to be repaid in full. But love your enemies, do good to them, and lend to them without expecting to get anything back. Then your reward will be great, and you will be sons of the Most High, because he is kind to the ungrateful and wicked. Be merciful, just as your Father is merciful." Luke 6:34-36

You must have accurate and honest weights and measures, so that you may live long in the land the Lord your God is giving you. Deuteronomy 25:15

Chapter 5—On guard!

Theme verse

"Watch out! Be on your guard against all kinds of greed; a man's life does not consist in the abundance of his possessions."
Luke 12:15

Chapter verses

Put to death, therefore, whatever belongs to your earthly nature: sexual immorality, impurity, lust, evil desires and greed, which is idolatry. Colossians 3:5

Jesus answered, "Everyone who drinks this water will be thirsty again, but whoever drinks the water I give him will never thirst. Indeed, the water I give him will become in him a spring of water welling up to eternal life. "The woman said to him, "Sir, give me this water so that I won't get thirsty and have to keep coming here to draw water." John 4:13-14

Do not wear yourself out to get rich; have the wisdom to show restraint. Cast but a glance at riches, and they are gone, for they will surely sprout wings and fly off to the sky like an eagle. Proverbs 23:4-5

And God spoke all these words: "I am the LORD your God, who brought you out of Egypt, out of the land of slavery. "You shall have no other gods before me. You shall not make for yourself an idol in the form of anything in heaven above or on the earth beneath or in the waters below. You shall not bow down to them or worship them; for I, the LORD your God, am a jealous God, punishing the children for the sin of the fathers to the third and fourth generation of those who hate me, but showing love to a thousand {generations} of those who love me and keep my commandments. You shall not misuse the name of the LORD your God, for the LORD will not hold anyone guiltless who misuses his name. Remember the Sabbath day by keeping it holy. Six days you shall labor and do all your work, but the seventh day is a Sabbath to the LORD your God. On it you shall not do any work, neither you, nor your son or daughter, nor your manservant or maidservant, nor your animals, nor the alien within your gates. For in six days the LORD made the heavens and the earth, the sea, and all that is in them, but he rested on the seventh day. Therefore the LORD blessed the Sabbath day and made it holy. Honor your father and your mother, so that you may live long in the land the LORD your God is giving you. "You shall not murder. You shall not commit adultery. You shall not steal. You shall not give false testimony against your neighbor. You shall not covet your neighbor's house. You shall not covet your neighbor's wife, or his manservant or maidservant, his ox or donkey, or anything that belongs to your neighbor. Exodus 20:1-17

And [Jesus] said to them, "Take heed and beware of covetousness, for one's life does not consist in the abundance of the things he possesses." Then He spoke a parable to them, saying: "The ground of a certain rich man yielded plentifully. And he thought within himself, saying, 'What shall I do, since I have no room to store my crops?' So he said, "I will do this: I will pull down my barns and build greater, and there I will store all my crops and my goods. And I will say to my soul, "Soul, you have many goods laid up for many years; take your ease; eat, drink, and be merry." But God said to him, "Fool! This night your soul will be required of you; then whose will those things be which you have provided?" So is he who lays up treasure for himself, and is not rich toward God." Luke 12:15-21 NKJV

And do not set your heart on what you will eat or drink; do not worry about it. For the pagan world runs after all such things, and your Father knows that you need them. But seek his kingdom, and these things will be given to you as well. Do not be afraid, little flock, for your Father has been pleased to give you the kingdom. Sell your possessions and give to the poor. Provide purses for yourselves that will not wear out, a treasure in heaven that will not be exhausted, where no thief comes near and no moth destroys. For where your treasure is, there your heart will be also. Luke 12:29-34

Then he said to them, "Watch out! Be on your guard against all kinds of greed; a man's life does not consist in the abundance of his possessions." Luke 12:15

"The thief comes only to steal, and to kill, and to destroy; I have come that they may have life, and have it more abundantly. John 10:10 NKJV

"Blessed are the poor in spirit, for theirs is the kingdom of heaven.
Blessed are those who mourn, for they will be comforted.
Blessed are the meek, for they will inherit the earth.
Blessed are those who hunger and thirst for righteousness, for they will be filled.
Blessed are the merciful, for they will be shown mercy.
Blessed are the pure in heart, for they will see God.
Blessed are the peacemakers, for they will be called sons of God.
Blessed are those who are persecuted because of righteousness, for theirs is the kingdom of heaven." Matthew 5:3-10

Blessed be the LORD, Who daily loads us with benefits. Psalm 68:19 NKJV

"This, then, is how you should pray: Our Father in heaven, hallowed be your name, your kingdom come, your will be done on earth as it is in heaven. Give us today our daily bread. Forgive us our debts, as we also have forgiven our debtors. And lead us not into temptation, but deliver us from the evil one." Matthew 6:9-12

"You cannot serve both God and Money. Therefore I tell you, do not worry about your life, what you will eat or drink; or about your body, what you will wear. Is not life more important than food, and the body more important than clothes? Look at the birds of the air; they do not sow or reap or store away in barns, and yet your heavenly Father feeds them. Are you not much more valuable than they? Who of you by worrying can add a single hour to his life? And why do you worry about clothes? See how the lilies of the field grow. They do not labor or spin. Yet I tell you that not even Solomon in all his splendor was dressed like one of these. If that is how God clothes the grass of the field, which is here today and tomorrow is thrown into the fire, will he not much more clothe you, O you of little faith? So do not worry, saying, 'What shall we eat?' or 'What shall we drink?' or 'What shall we wear?' For the pagans run after all these things, and your heavenly Father knows that you need them. But seek first his kingdom and his righteousness, and all these things will be given to you as well." Matthew 6:24-33

"Any of you who does not give up everything he has cannot be my disciple." Luke 14:33

Chapter 6—Jesus Claus ain't coming to town?

Theme verse

"By . . . hard work we must help the weak, remembering the words the Lord Jesus himself said:
It is more blessed to give than to receive." Acts 20:35

Chapter verses

The people rejoiced at the willing response of their leaders, for they had given freely and wholeheartedly to the LORD. David the king also rejoiced greatly. 1 Chronicles 29:9

This is how we've come to understand and experience love: Christ sacrificed his life for us. This is why we ought to live sacrificially for our fellow believers, and not just be out for ourselves. If you see some brother or sister in need and have the means to do something about it but turn a cold shoulder and do nothing, what happens to God's love? It disappears. And you made it disappear. My dear children, let's not just talk about love; let's practice real love. This is the only way we'll know we're living truly, living in God's reality. 1 John 3:16-19 THE MESSAGE

As he taught, Jesus said, "Watch out for the teachers of the law. They like to walk around in flowing robes and be greeted in the marketplaces, and have the most important seats in the synagogues and the places of honor at banquets. They devour widows' houses and for a show make lengthy prayers. Such men will be punished most severely." Jesus sat down opposite the place where the offerings were put and watched the crowd putting their money into the temple treasury. Many rich people threw in large amounts. But a poor widow came and put in two very small copper coins, worth only a fraction of a penny. Calling his disciples to him, Jesus said, "I tell you the truth, this poor widow has put more into the treasury than all the others. They all gave out of their wealth; but she, out of her poverty, put in everything—all she had to live on." Mark 12:38-44

Though I speak with the tongues of men and of angels, and have not charity, I am become as sounding brass, or a tinkling cymbal. And though I have the gift of prophecy, and understand all mysteries, and all knowledge; and though I have all faith, so that I could remove mountains, and have not charity, I am nothing. And though I bestow all my goods to feed the poor, and though I give my body to be burned, and have not charity, it profiteth me nothing. . . . And now abideth faith, hope, charity, these three; but the greatest of these is charity. 1 Corinthians 13:1-3,13 KJV

Give to the one who asks you, and do not turn away from the one who wants to borrow from you. Matthew 5:42

Let each one [give] as he has made up his own mind and purposed in his heart, not reluctantly or sorrowfully or under compulsion, for God loves (He takes pleasure in, prizes above other things, and is unwilling to abandon or to do without) a cheerful (joyous, "prompt to do it") giver [whose heart is in his giving]. 2 Corinthians 9:7 THE AMPLIFIED

He who is kind to the poor lends to the LORD, and he will reward him for what he has done. Proverbs 19:17

John answered, "The man with two tunics should share with him who has none, and the one who has food should do the same." Luke 3:11

Give, and it will be given to you. A good measure, pressed down, shaken together and running over, will be poured into your lap. For with the measure you use, it will be measured to you." Luke 6:38

Sell your possessions and give to the poor. Provide purses for yourselves that will not wear out, a treasure in heaven that will not be exhausted, where no thief comes near and no moth destroys. Luke 12:33

"No one can serve two masters. Either he will hate the one and love the other, or he will be devoted to the one and despise the other. You cannot serve both God and Money. Matthew 6:24

Jesus looked at him and loved him. "One thing you lack," he said. "Go, sell everything you have and give to the poor, and you will have treasure in heaven. Then come, follow me." Mark 10:21

The entire law is summed up in a single command: "Love your neighbor as yourself." Galatians 5:14

Additional References

"If I have put my trust in gold or said to pure gold, 'You are my security,' if I have rejoiced over my great wealth, the fortune my hands had gained, if I have regarded the sun in its radiance or the moon moving in splendor, so that my heart was secretly enticed and my hand offered them a kiss of homage, then these also would be sins to be judged, for I would have been unfaithful to God on high." Job 31:24-28

Do not be overawed when a man grows rich, when the splendor of his house increases; for he will take nothing with him when he dies, his splendor will not descend with him. Though while he lived he counted himself blessed—and men praise you when you prosper—he will join the generation of his fathers, who will never see the light of life. Psalm 49:16-19

Wealth is worthless in the day of wrath, but righteousness delivers from death. Proverbs 11:4

Whoever trusts in his riches will fall, but the righteous will thrive like a green leaf. Proverbs 11:28

The faithful man will be richly blessed, but one eager to get rich will not go unpunished. Proverbs 28:20

Give me neither poverty nor riches, but give me only my daily bread. Otherwise, I may have too much and disown you and say, "Who is the LORD?" Or I may become poor and steal, and so dishonor the name of my God. Proverbs 30:8-9

Keep your lives free from the love of money and be content with what you have, because God has said, "Never will I leave you; never will I forsake you." Hebrews 13:5

"They have become rich and powerful and have grown fat and sleek... they do not plead the case of the fatherless to win it, they do not defend the rights of the poor. Should I not punish them for this?" declares the Lord. Jeremiah 5:27-29

"Do not store up for yourselves treasures on earth, where moth and rust destroy, and where thieves break in and steal. But store up for yourselves treasures in heaven, where moth and rust do not destroy, and where thieves do not break in and steal. For where your treasure is, there your heart will be also." Matthew 6:19-21

Still others, like seed sown among thorns, hear the word; but the worries of this life, the deceitfulness of wealth and the desires for other things come in and choke the word, making it unfruitful. Mark 4:18-19

What good is it for a man to gain the whole world, yet lose or forfeit his very self? Luke 9:25

[Angel speaking to Cornelius] "Your prayers and gifts to the poor have come up as a memorial offering before God." Acts 10:5

All the believers were together and had everything in common. Selling their possessions and goods, they gave to anyone as he had need. Acts 2:44-45

"That servant who knows his master's will and does not get ready or does not do what his master wants will be beaten with many blows. But the one who does not know and does things deserving punishment will be beaten with few blows. From everyone who has been given much, much will be demanded; and from the one who has been entrusted with much, much more will be asked." Luke 12:47-48

"When you give a luncheon or a dinner, do not invite your friends, your brothers or relatives, or your rich neighbors; if you do, they may invite you back and so you will be repaid. But when you give a banquet, invite the poor, the crippled, the lame, the blind, and you will be blessed. Although they cannot repay you, you will be repaid at the resurrection of the righteous." Luke 14:12-14

"There was a rich man who was dressed in purple and fine linen and lived in luxury every day. At his gate was laid a beggar named Lazarus, covered with sores and longing to eat what fell from the rich man's table. Even the dogs came and licked his sores. The time came when the beggar died and the angels carried him to Abraham's side. The rich man also died and was buried. In hell, where he was in torment, he looked up and saw Abraham far away, with Lazarus by his side. So he called to him, 'Father Abraham, have pity on me and send Lazarus to dip the tip of his finger in water and cool my tongue, because I am in agony in this fire.' "But Abraham replied, 'Son, remember that in your lifetime you received your good things, while Lazarus received bad things, but now he is comforted here and you are in agony. And besides all this, between us and you a great chasm has been fixed, so that those who want to go from here to you cannot, nor can anyone cross over from there to us.' "He answered, 'Then I beg you, father, send Lazarus to my father's house, for I have five brothers. Let him warn them, so that they will not also come to this place of torment.' "Abraham replied, 'They have Moses and the Prophets; let them listen to them.' " 'No, father Abraham,' he said, 'but if someone from the dead goes to them, they will repent.' "He said to him, 'If they do not listen to Moses and the Prophets, they will not be convinced even if someone rises from the dead.' " Luke 16:19-31

But godliness with contentment is great gain. For we brought nothing into the world, and we can take nothing out of it. But if we have food and clothing, we will be content with that. People who want to get rich fall into temptation and a trap and into many foolish and harmful desires that plunge men into ruin and destruction. But if we have food and clothing, we will be content with that. People who want to get rich fall into temptation and a trap and into many foolish and harmful desires that plunge men into ruin and destruction. For the love of money is a root of all kinds of evil. Some people, eager for money, have wandered from the faith and pierced themselves with many griefs. But you, man of God, flee from all this, and pursue righteousness, godliness, faith, love, endurance and gentleness. 1 Timothy 6:6-11

Command those who are rich in this present world not to be arrogant nor to put their hope in wealth, which is so uncertain, but to put their hope in God, who richly provides us with everything for our enjoyment. Command them to do good, to be rich in good deeds, and to be generous and willing to share. In this way they will lay up treasure for themselves as a firm foundation for the coming age, so that they may take hold of the life that is truly life. 1 Timothy 6:17-19

"Remember the Lord your God, for it is he who gives you the ability to produce wealth."
Deuteronomy 8:18

. . . I have learned to be content whatever the circumstances. I know what it is to be in need, and I know what it is to have plenty. I have learned the secret of being content in any and every situation, whether well fed or hungry, whether living in plenty or in want. I can do everything through him who gives me strength. Philippians 4:11-13

Now you should carry this project through to completion just as enthusiastically as you began it. Give whatever you can according to what you have. If you are really eager to give, it isn't important how much you are able to give. God wants you to give what you have, not what you don't have. 2 Corinthians 8:11-12 NLT

But just as you excel in everything—in faith, in speech, in knowledge, in complete earnestness and in your love for us—see that you also excel in this grace of giving. 2 Corinthians 8:7

Now he who supplies seed to the sower and bread for food will also supply and increase your store of seed and will enlarge the harvest of your righteousness. You will be made rich in every way so that you can be generous on every occasion, and through us your generosity will result in thanksgiving to God. This service that you perform is not only supplying the needs of God's people but is also overflowing in many expressions of thanks to God. Because of the service by which you have proved yourselves, men will praise God for the obedience that accompanies your confession of the gospel of Christ, and for your generosity in sharing with them and with everyone else. 2 Corinthians 9:10-13

May those who delight in my vindication shout for joy and gladness; may they always say, "The LORD be exalted, who delights in the well-being of his servant." Psalm 35:27

You say, 'I am rich; I have acquired wealth and do not need a thing.' But you do not realize that you are wretched, pitiful, poor, blind and naked. I counsel you to buy from me gold refined in the fire, so you can become rich; and white clothes to wear, so you can cover your shameful nakedness; and salve to put on your eyes, so you can see. Those whom I love I rebuke and discipline. So be earnest, and repent. Revelation 3:17-19

IN GOD WE TRUST

CD-204009 *Taking Godly Care of My Money*

Answer Key

Page 12
1. God
2. the environment
   our bodies
   gold and silver, or money
3. Currency, coins, credit cards, checks
4. Answers will vary.

Page 16
Across
2. Levites
5. tithe
6. dwelling

Down
1. aliens
3. exchange
4. steward

Page 26
Answers will vary.

Page 27

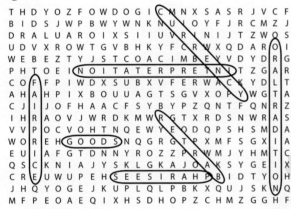

Page 32
Answers will vary.

Page 35

Page 36
1. C
2. E
3. G
4. H
5. A
6. B
7. I
8. J
9. D
10. F
11. K

Page 44
Answers will vary.

Page 47
1. debt
2. credit
3. euphemism
4. revenue
5. long-term
6. expenses
7. interest
8. usury
9. budget
10. compound
11. fair trade

"You must have **accurate** and **honest** weights and measures, so that you may **live long** in the land the LORD you God is giving you."

Page 53
1. He built barns to store grain and goods.
2. He stored in barns so that he would know he had plenty stored up for many years.
3. He thought he would take life easy; eat, drink, and be merry.
4. banks, credit unions, stocks, bonds, etc.
5. Answers will vary.

Page 57
Answers will vary.

Page 58
Answers will vary.

Page 60
Across
3. materialism
5. slogan
6. greed

Down
1. possessions
2. blessed
4. abundant

Page 69
1. charity
2. cheerful
3. give
4. grudging
5. sacrifice

"Love your neighbor as yourself."

CD-204009 *Taking Godly Care of My Money*